WHOLE FOOT REVOLUTION

A Proven Way to Reclaim Your Mind, Body, and Sole

DR. ANTHONY WEINERT

DreamSculpt Books & Media

Library of Congress – In Process

Published in the USA by:
DreamSculpt Books
www.DreamSculpt.com
an imprint of Waterside Productions
2055 Oxford Ave.
Cardiff by the Sea, CA. 92007
Waterside.com

Printed in the United States of America

First Printing, 2019

ISBNs
978-1-943625-94-9 print edition
978-1-943625-95-6 ebook edition

DEDICATION

Dedicated to the loving memory of my beautiful mother, Diane Weinert.

I truly miss her every day but know she is with me in spirit guiding me along my life path and journey. I am so blessed and honored to have been able to have such a wonderful, supportive and loving mother.

She always inspired me to work hard and to dream big and not to let anyone tell me that I can't do something. She would always tell me to be the best that I can be and to never lose focus on my goals and dreams in life.

www.WholeFootRevolution.com

TABLE OF CONTENTS

ACKNOWLEDGEMENTS

I would like to acknowledge and thank all of those people who have contributed and helped me with the completion of *Whole Foot Revolution.*

A very special thank you to my amazing wife, Julie, who is my soulmate and love of my life. You are such a wonderful wife, mother and friend and I am so blessed to have you in my life. I appreciate all your support and guidance during the writing of my book.

I also want to thank my son Evan, whom I am so proud of and so blessed to have in my life. I appreciate you always giving me encouragement and being understanding of my time during the writing of my book. You mean the world to me and I love you so much.

I also want to thank my dog Bo, for always being there for me during the early mornings and late nights during the writing of my book. Thank you for always being there to give me love and put a smile on my face during the times I needed it the most. You truly are my best friend and I love you so much.

I also want to acknowledge and thank my dad, Norbert, for giving me the strength and willingness to keep going with my book and not give up. I am so blessed to have you as my father and appreciate all you have done for me. Your words of encouragement mean a lot to me and I thank you for always supporting me. I love you so much.

Special thanks and gratitude to both Jared Rosen and Lynn Kitchen whom encouraged me and committed many hours in helping me fulfill my dream and vision of this revolutionary book. I thank you both for always being there for me as a mentor and friend. I feel so blessed and honored to have you both in my life. Thank you both for being on my team and for all your wisdom and support.

I would also like to give thanks and gratitude to Bill Gladstone and Waterside for giving me the opportunity to have my revolutionary book published and allow readers to reclaim their mind, body, and sole.

I also want to thank all of my teachers and mentors for allowing me to open up my mind to other methods and forms of integrative healing and the important role our feet have in our overall health and wellness. Thank you, Laura Norman for allowing me to see how the feet are a true mirror to our body and health wellness and teaching me all about Reflexology.

Thank you Grandmaster Nan Lu, Elaine, and Traditional Chinese Medicine World Foundation for opening up my mind to alternative healing modalities and teaching me all about Meridians,

Qi, and the healing of our bodies through Traditional Chinese Medicine.

I want to also thank Tom Tam, his son Bell, and his daughter Yvonne for allowing me to see a new world of healing through bioelectricity, Tong Ren and Quantum Healing. I thank you all for all your wonderful trainings and teachings. I will be forever thankful as you opened up my mind to new ways of healing and made me truly understand the true root cause of diseases and illnesses.

I also want to thank my friend Chuck Christian who is such an inspiration to me. He is not only a talented artist, former University of Michigan football player, but he also healed himself from stage 4 cancer utilizing Tong Ren Quantum Healing. I appreciate you contributing your story to my book and how it may help other readers who may be dealing with similar situations. You truly are a Superman. Your positive attitude love of life, strength, and willingness to help others is absolutely amazing. I am so honored and blessed to have you in my life and appreciate all you do.

INTRODUCTION

For many thousands of years, people walked barefoot or wore make-shift foot coverings, and used herbs, plants, and oils to heal their feet. Since the advent of mass-produced shoes and modern civilization, feet are often covered in synthetic socks and rubber soled shoes that too infrequently touch the earth. Wearing shoes has distinct advantages, but I hope to show you why focusing attention on our feet, aligning them, caring for them, and letting them touch the earth is something old as time and yet very revolutionary today.

In *Whole Foot Revolution*, you will learn a lot about feet and how important they are to your overall well-being and happiness. You will learn that the structure of the foot goes beyond its bones and muscles but is part of an intricate network of nerves that continually communicates with the brain and other organs. You will learn that neglecting your feet can create problems that can adversely affect your overall health.

As you read from chapter to chapter, you will discover a new way of looking at and relating to those two body parts that carry you through your day. This revolutionary perspective is the result of many years of study that came initially from my Western medical education and later from my immersion into traditional Chinese medicine. My knowledge and fascination with bioelectricity, quantum healing, gravity healing, and the future of foot health has added to my journey. This path to holistic health has in some ways been long, but in other ways, it has been only a little step towards the transformation of the sole of the world.

As a child, I always wanted to know answers to questions and would always ask, "why, why, why?" As a physician and surgeon, I had many patients suffering from diseases and illness which was very frustrating for me. I wondered why some people take so long to heal? That is what made me want to learn other modalities to treat patients appropriately.

OLD SHOES

As a kid growing up, I was really into sports. I wanted to play soccer, but could not afford to get new cleats, so I wore hand-me-downs from my older brother. Not realizing that his shoes had worn out to accommodate his misalignments, I began to have some pain in the bottom of my foot and into the heel area where I experienced sharp, jabbing, stabbing knife-like pain that shot up into my heel. Every morning the pain started when I got out of bed. It was a nagging pain that never went away, and affected my daily activities making me very cranky and miserable.

Eventually, I saw a foot specialist who diagnosed my condition as plantar fasciitis. After treatment, I realized how much pain affects moods and every day activity. Since we depend on our feet all the time, foot pain is debilitating for young and old.

At a young age, I knew I wanted to go into medicine because I had a passion for helping people and that has never changed. I realize how important the foot is and how it affects kids as well as the older population. In addition, I work with a lot of professional athletes who have a high percentage of foot and ankle issues from playing sports, and I realize that as our overall population becomes more athletic–engaging in walking, marathons, and daily aerobic activity–more people will have to start paying attention to their feet if they want to stay healthy and happy.

My passion is to educate my patients and readers about the importance of their feet, and that is why I wrote *Whole Foot Revolution*. The title conveys a new, holistic, state-of-the-art approach to foot care that affects our whole self. Moreover, there is even more to the story of my passion for helping others with their feet.

MEET MY MOM

My mother grew up in a family of fifteen kids. Her parents were Polish immigrants who lived in Hamtramck, Michigan. They were very poor during those years. Because there were so many kids in the family, they all wore hand me down shoes from one sibling to another. My mom often said that growing up they had shoes that did not fit. Most of the shoes had holes in them. Many of the shoes were so worn down that the top cover was hanging off from the sole.

Sometimes my mom even walked to school barefoot. She worked at a church during her teen years, and she and her siblings often had their only real meals there. So, she lived through an impoverished financial childhood! Years ago, when reflecting on her life, she often mentioned that we should feel blessed that we have shoes to wear. She had many stories about all the foot problems that her family endured because of shoes that did not fit to their feet.

Wearing other people's shoes that have adapted to the original owner can cause more harm than good in many ways. Of course, if it is snowing or cold, it is important to have anything on your feet to protect them, but in this time of prosperity in the world—and particularly in the United States—it is a tragedy that we do not know how important our feet are.

My medical practice is in Michigan, and for many years I have been troubled by the many homeless walking around Detroit who have ill-fitting shoes with holes and damp socks. As I travel the country, I see the same situation in both warm and cold climates. While some might think that there are more significant issues with the homeless or low-income families than their feet, I disagree! Our feet are the literal foundation of our body, mind, and spirit.

Resulting from this suffering with both patients and the homeless, I started a non-profit called *Shoe Pantry Plus*, a 501c3 that distributes new, properly fitting shoes and socks to those who need them. New shoes are important because as we walk the shoe adapts to our gait and that will prevent problems with the feet, and it will also help prevent issues with the knees, hips, back and the entire musculoskeletal chain. I believe that those living with less than adequate financial resources will thrive in many ways by having shoes that fit. They will be healthier and happier, and that can result in doing better in school as a kid or getting a better job as an adult. In my opinion, everyone deserves properly fitting, new shoes.

So back to my inspiration about starting *Shoe Pantry Plus*. My mom had a rare blood disorder called amyloidosis in which abnormal proteins in the blood eventually shut down the organs, so she went to Mayo Clinic for a stem cell transplant. Amyloidosis is very rare and not too many people, including physicians, know what it is including myself when my mom was first diagnosed. I had to do a lot of research on the internet about Amyloidosis and fortunately was able to find Dr. Gertz, who was an amyloidosis specialist at the Mayo Clinic to help my mom. However, recently in 2018 it has become more visible to the public eye when celebrity public figure Matt Millen was diagnosed. Matt Millen was a 4-time Super Bowl Champion in the NFL and also was President and CEO of my beloved hometown Detroit Lions from 2001-2008. He then served as NFL and college football broadcast analyst for various networks including ESPN, Fox, and Big Ten Network.

This very rare blood disorder hits home for me, especially because my mom was diagnosed and was able to battle through it with her strong will and faith and was able to get her amyloidosis in remission. She was doing very well after the transplant, but later she slipped and fell down the steps of her house. She went to the emergency room for her fall, but unfortunately, they were not experienced with amyloidosis, and she developed complications.

She ended up needing dialysis because she was going downhill with her kidneys. She also developed lung issues and other problems. While helping her through that tough time, I developed the vision to create a non-profit focused on distributing shoes to help adults and children so that they do not have to endure what my mom had to endure while growing up. As a foot specialist today,

I find it befitting to offer my medical practice to professional athletes, dancers, and the public, while also supporting a non-profit that distributes new, properly fitting shoes and socks to the poor and homeless.

After my mom passed away in 2011, I eventually created *Shoe Pantry Plus*. The logo for *Shoe Pantry Plus* is a pair of shoes that my son painted when he was eight years old. The angel wings that carry the shoes signifies my mom who would want everyone to have properly fitting shoes and socks. I carry that burden for her.

When the non-profit first started, we were invited to an event called the "Backyard Barbeque" that was really cool. It was for the homeless at the Eastern Market in Detroit. The organizers heard about my passion from an interview I did on WJR radio and they got in touch with me at last minute before the event. They asked if I would be willing to come and give shoes out to the homeless. I said, "yeah I will come there, but I do not have a big supply of shoes." Since it was winter and I did not yet have an organized foundation, so I ended up buying 200 pairs of boots for men, women, and children, and I prayed that we had the right sizes for those who showed up.

As it turned out from that early learning experience, some of the people that wanted boots did not get them. I did not have enough of them, and I only had small quantities of specific sizes. As people lined up, I would guess their foot size and distribute what we had, along with a pair of socks in little drawstring backpacks. We went through 200 pairs within an hour or so, and that was when I realized that I had to work even harder to do good in this world. In the future, my dream with the foundation is to own mobile trucks that drive directly to those on the streets in need as well as to shelters, soup kitchens, or schools with measuring devices and other medical supplies so that we can distribute proper shoes and socks to those in need. Did you know that many homeless do not know their shoe size? Also, children and teens in these circumstances are often never fitted because they can't afford to shop in shoe stores. They wear whatever is handed down to them.

Me and my dad (Norbert).

I am fortunate and blessed to be a foot surgeon and to have a good life and family. It is my opinion that we need to help one another out, while we take care of our feet. The *Whole Foot Revolution* is based on the knowledge that we are holistic beings—and everything from our feet to our brains—and everyone from the rich to the poor—are entangled in one way or another. In other words, we are all "One" in this universe. It's time to change the world, one sole at a time.

I truly believe that *"Whole Foot Revolution"* will open people's minds to revolutionary ideas and healing principles that will help to transform their lives. Throughout *"Whole Foot Revolution"* you will find out how important your feet are to your overall health wellness and how they are a mirror to your body, mind, and spirit.

As you read through the chapters you will experience the healing and energy power of the earth through the soles of your feet and the "oneness" you will feel with your mind, body and soul. Let's all live the *"Whole Foot Revolution"* together and be sure to share your experiences and stories with us on our website www.whole-footrevolution.com

Chapter One:

THE MIRACULOUS FOOT

The human foot is a masterpiece of
engineering and a work of art.
Leonardo da Vinci

THE WEIGHT OF THE WORLD

The foot is one of the most important parts of our entire body. It carries the weight of our entire body, is incredibly complex, and endures a lifetime of weight and pressure. The American Podiatric Medical Association (APMA) website estimates that the average person will have walked 75,000 miles by age 50 demonstrating the amazing power of our feet since many of us will live to be in our 80s and beyond and *still* walking. Each foot has 26 bones, 33 joints, 19 muscles and 107 ligaments that come together to hold our weight and the conditions underfoot. Our feet contain a quarter of the bones that we have in our entire body! And what most of us experience if we run in the summer and take off our shoes, each foot has 250,000 sweat glands and our feet can produce half pint of moisture a day.

The feet are the most sensitive area of the body. Because of the sensitivity created by thousands of nerve fiber endings, prisoners were tortured for centuries with techniques that inflicted intense pain and suffering to the feet. Foot whipping–or bastinado–was a method of corporal punishment dating back thousands of years in many cultures around the world, in which special instruments were developed to whip the bottoms of prisoner's feet. A deeply dreaded form of torture, the pain of this form of whipping was worse than flogging the backs of prisoners. Some other forms of torture with the feet includes placing extreme heat like a hot iron to the bottom of the bare soles or crushing the foot with instruments like a Spanish boot, Malay boot, or foot press.

Foot binding was an ancient Chinese custom inflicted upon women in China from about the 10th century and ended in 1911 to keep their feet tiny, which was esthetically pleasing to men. All the bones in the feet were broken except the big toe. The feet were then bandaged in such a way that bent their toes towards the heel to keep their feet tiny. For centuries, the Chinese believed the beauty of tiny feet was even more important than the face. Not only did foot binding cause a lot of pain for these women, but it also affected the entire body causing deformities, walking gait issues, and many medical problems.

Rarely contemplated today is that the bottoms of our feet have over 7,000 nerves–more nerve endings than any other part of our body. That might explain why when we tickle our kids' feet, it can be almost unbearable! And why as adults, foot massage can be so pleasant.

The feet also carry great symbolic meaning in many cultures. Our feet connect our minds and bodies to the earth and carry metaphors such as "being grounded" or "having one's feet planted firmly on the ground." In ancient mythology, Mother Earth resided in the soil, and devotees walked barefoot to show respect (*Book of Symbols*, p. 424). In many cultures, the disciple washed or kissed the feet of the master to show respect and love. Symbols of sensuality, feet are often massaged with oils and adorned with beautiful sandals and manicured nails. They act as resilient instruments of sports and the arts, carrying athletes through hours of competitive sports, and dancers through ballet and performances.

It is estimated that over 75% of the population have problems with their feet (as cited from the APMA website) whether properly diagnosed or not. And even more interesting is that the feet—and particularly the nerves in the feet—can be used to diagnose and heal other organs in the body very effectively.

The 7,000 nerve fiber endings
in the bottom of each foot, or
14,000 total foot nerves act as an
information highway running from
our feet through our organs.

The 7,000 nerve fiber endings in the bottom of each foot, or 14,000 total foot nerves act as an information highway running from our feet through our organs. These nerves keep us coordinated and in balance by firing impulses that communicate directly with the brain. The information coming in from our feet directs the tiny muscular and soft tissue tendons to help us maintain balance and coordination when we walk and when we run. Energy also comes in through the soles of our feet which you will learn a lot more about in the coming chapters.

The soles of our feet are very intricate, with many pressure points that link those points to pathways that connect to specific organs, glands and parts of our body such as shoulders, arms and legs. As many who have studied reflexology, acupuncture, or foot massage know, the soles of our feet are very important to our overall body, health and wellness. The *American Podiatric Medical Association* states that the average day of walking brings a force that is equal to several thousand tons our feet. This partly explains why our feet are more subject to injury than any other part of our body, and why our nerves feel frayed when our feet are not happy.

STICK'S STORY

I worked with a homeless gentleman Alexander, nicknamed "Sticks" by his friend because he was tall and slender. I met him in May 2017 at a homeless shelter in Detroit and he was eating at a table all by himself. I approached him, introduced myself, and asked him if he needed some new shoes and socks and he was hesitant to talk. He finally opened up and said he would love a new pair of shoes as the shoes he is wearing are too small for him. I then measured his feet with a Brannock device and noticed 2 eye opening things. Number one is that his foot size was a men's 13 and he was wearing a shoe that was a men's 12 which is a full size small.

The second thing I noticed was that he had no socks on. When questioned, he stated that he doesn't wear socks because it makes his shoes too tight and he can't put them on. I then went to get him his new pair of size 13 men's shoes and also a pair of socks. He then tried them on and his whole demeanor changed. He had a smile on his face and was so appreciative and gave me a big hug and thanked me. He said he can finally walk without pain. I was so happy that he started to open up to me. He told me that he used to be an attorney and his daughter died suddenly in a car accident. He then said that 5 months after his daughter died, his wife died suddenly of a brain aneurysm.

He was so depressed and said he wanted to end his life. He couldn't do his job as an attorney any more as he was so depressed and started drinking heavy alcohol and then got into drugs. He didn't pay any of his bills and eventually lost his home. I had so much empathy for him and gave him a big hug on the losses of both his wife and daughter and told him everything will be ok. He told me that it was so nice for him to see that there really are people out there that care and that treat him like any normal person. When I spoke with Sticks he said that he feels alone in this world now without his wife and daughter whom he loved so much. He said that he would eventually like to go to rehab and get his life back together, so he can go back into being an attorney—the profession he loved prior to the loss of the two people he loved the most.

I talked to him about the power of the mind and how it can heal his body. I also told him about meditation and grounding to help him with his depression, stress, and anxiety. I wanted him to know there are people out there that really care about him and that we are all brothers and sisters in this world. After our talk, I could see the twinkle in his eye and the attitude change of wanting to get better. I then went back to the homeless shelter in November of 2017 to help distribute new shoes and socks and asked where Sticks was. I was told that he went to rehab in June and they had not seen him at the shelter since that time. I was so happy that he took the leap to go to rehab and better himself and his life as he has too many precious gifts and attributes to contribute to this world.

This is a pure example on how we as human beings should never pass judgement on anyone, especially those who are homeless. You never know what people are going through in their lives and what truly is their life story. We have to be compassionate towards others and most importantly spread more love in this world. There is too much hatred and negativity in this world which I believe is causing a lot of stress and a lot more diseases and illnesses. Fear and emotions get in the way of a lot of people in this world. Our mind is a powerful healer to us all and if we can focus on being positive, showing compassion, and most importantly loving one another, this world will be a better place.

THE STEPS WE TAKE

Our feet have a big role to play in carrying us through life. Throughout history we were very dependent on our feet whether we were working in the fields or walking to fetch some water to drink. Many people in Africa and other third world countries walk miles on their feet to get food and water. In today's culture, we utilize transportation with cars and other motorized vehicles and don't walk as much as we did earlier in history.

We have become a society that is dependent on transportation vehicles. The average American walk to their garage and drive to an office, go up and down in elevators and rarely touches the earth with their feet. For those living in cities without cars they have more choices for getting around than ever, beyond public transportations with services like Uber, Lyft to get them places. In addition, in today's world, especially in the downtown and college campuses, they now have electric scooters that you can rent and ride to get you around town instead of walking.

A sedentary person takes about 1,000 to 3,000 steps per day, and an active person could more than ten thousand steps. That's a lot of weight and strain that we place on our feet every day, and the more weight we carry the more pressure we put on the feet. As most of us know, losing a few extra pounds not only helps our heart and our ego, but it also takes pressure off our very sensitive feet. I will be sharing more about diet and weight in a coming chapter, but for now remember that we want our feet to last a lifetime, so we must take care of them!

FOOT NOTES

Rub for Rub

After a hard day of work, I am sure you would love to have your feet rubbed. Many times, when we exchange foot rubs with a spouse or friend we don't fully appreciate the experience as we anticipate reciprocating. Here is a fun exercise that will give two people a shared experience.

Take your shoes and socks off and allow your feet to breath and rub each other's feet at the same time.

If they push in a particular area, push exactly in the same area as they as to you and just tell each other how you feel and what your experiencing.

You will be amazed at how fun and therapeutic this will be not only to yourself, but the increased bond and closeness you will feel towards each other and become "one" with each other.

CARRYING THE BURDEN

Three out of four Americans will experience serious foot issues in their lifetime, many of which are treatable as well as preventable. The feet are truly the foundation to our entire musculoskeletal system. That is a lot of responsibility resting on two feet and that is why it is so important to consider new and revolutionary approaches to health that starts and ends with the feet.

When our feet are out of alignment, we will likely develop problems with our ankles, knees, hips, lower back, shoulders, jaw, head, and with our mood.

When our feet are out of alignment, we will likely develop problems with our ankles, knees, hips, lower back, shoulders, jaw, head, and with our mood. Being out of alignment is an attributing cause of health issues that many people do not realize. Many would never consider feet as a primary cause of other aches and pains. I have seen patients spend thousands of dollars getting massages or chiropractic adjustments for back or shoulder pain without realizing that their misaligned feet were the basis of the problem. And while massage and chiropractors are a wonderful health support, it really doesn't help until your feet are in alignment. Since one quarter of our body's bones are in our feet, any misalignment of those particular bones can cause trouble in the rest of the body. You'll read more about foot alignment in Chapter 6.

In my opinion, our feet are the most abused part of our body. We often care about what our shoes look like and we spend a lot of money looking fashionable while neglecting what is inside. And in today's active society where we often spend many hours a week running or playing tennis or doing yoga–and even standing at our desks which is the newest trend to overcome hours of daily sitting. After a hard day at work our feet are often crying for attention, begging to be rubbed, but the most many of us do is "put them up" while we watch TV in the evening. Carrying our body's weight for 8 or 10 hours a day, our feet need support to keep the musculoskeletal system in balance and to influence our mood and mind, so leaning new approaches to foot care is critical.

THE CHICKEN AND THE EGG

With an epidemic of obesity in the USA (NCBI, 2018) and a growing interest in anti-aging and longevity, people might know the value of walking and other exercise, but very often pain stops people from being consistent. Primary care doctors often suggest daily walking to lose weight (along with diet control) and many try to follow this advice, but foot pain stops them. There is a "chicken and egg" phenomenon that occurs when the feet hurt so we sometimes don't use them as much as we should, and yet it is the feet that will ultimately get us back to good health. Being overweight increases the odds of developing diabetes, high cholesterol, high blood pressure, cancer, and heart disease.

If a person is suffering with pain while they walk due to weight issues, they may need to find some alternative ways to exercise their feet. Even sitting on a chair and moving your feet daily is better than not doing anything. You can even get a small foot spa jet tub and put your feet in it and move your feet while the water and jets help increase the blood flow and circulation to your feet. I would even suggest you add a few tablespoons of Epsom salt to the water and this will help to detox your body.

For those people dealing with weight issues and struggling with pain while they walk, I would suggest you start off slow and eventually increase a little more walking each day. I would even suggest this little exercise for you to do at the house in the comfort of your own home.

First, take off your shoes and socks and then sit in a comfortable chair. Then put your feet on the ground and close your eyes and visualize you are walking around the neighborhood. As you are visualizing, move your feet up and down like you are physically walking and so that your feet are touching the ground and as the one foot is on the ground, your other foot is up off the ground. I would do this virtual sitting exercise for a total of 15 minutes. Feel free to even put some headphones on and listen to music or whatever you wish to make the time go by fast just as if you were actually walking. Doing these little exercises 1-2 times a day will do wonders for your health and best of all, these baby steps will eventually lead you to eventually building up to more walking and more steps which will lead to a happier, healthier, and enriching life.

FOOT NOTES

Sitting Feet Exercise

Here is a great exercise you can do at home to help strengthen and work your foot muscles is the following.

Sit in a comfortable chair and take off your shoes and socks. Bring your right foot out a little bit and then start to do the alphabet with your toes on your feet.

Pretend your toes are writing on a piece of paper. After you do the alphabet from A to Z with the right foot, then switch to your left foot and do the same thing with the alphabet from A to Z. Be sure to say the letter you are doing out loud and I would do a total of 3 complete sets for both feet.

PAYING ATTENTION

I always find it interesting that when a patient visits a primary care physician for examination, very few actually examine the feet. Particularly with diabetic patients, the feet are an essential area to look at and evaluate because the feet tell you everything about the body. The feet inform us of diseases, illnesses, the source of pain, circulation issues, or many body ailments because the foot is a literal mirror to the body. As a foot doctor for over 20 years, I continue to be fascinated by the extraordinary body parts that hold us up. I have come to truly appreciate why I am a medical doctor focused on the feet.

Many of my patients suffer with plantar fascitis and heel pain that is common for runners. Many footballers get ankle sprains and also toe conditions–some of which is caused from trauma–but many of these conditions are preventable with proper foot care. We also often see sesamoidoitis in dancers and also fractures in certain sports like soccer, many of which are preventable. And we treat many "weekend injuries" that occur primarily in parents playing basketball with their kids or their friends and they rupture their Achilles tendon. I am not saying that every foot problem or injury is preventable, but I will say that a high percentage of suffering could be alleviated if more people understood their feet.

More than 100 million individuals have diabetes in the United States alone. I urge my diabetic patients to take good care of their feet because diabetics run into risk of amputations or gangrene.

This book is not intended to tell you all the horror stories of the medical industry, but I do want to make the point more than once that if we can help ourselves prevent serious health issues by paying more attention to our feet we will all live longer and happier lives. And of course, when patients do have problems, helping them get back on their feet is really rewarding, and that is one of the reasons that I picked this specialty when I decided to become a doctor. I truly love and love helping change the quality of life for patients by educating them on how important the feet.

FOOT NOTES

Sitting Foot Exercise

Here is also another great and fun exercise you can do with your feet and it is very fun to help with the strengthening of your muscles in your feet and toes. You can even have a contest with your partner if you would like.

First you want to get a bunch of marbles and put them on the ground. You then want to get a big bucket and put it to the side of you while you are sitting in a comfortable chair.

Then start with your right foot and grab some marbles with your toes and then drop them into the bucket using your feet only. After you drop the marbles into the bucket, then do the same thing with your left foot. Keep rotating feet and continue until all the marbles are in the bucket.

You can make it even more fun if you had a partner to do the exercise and they would need to have their own bucket and same amount of marbles as you. Then say go and whoever can fill their bucket up first with the marbles will be the winner. There are so many creative exercises you can do with your feet and best of all it is so great for your health and wellness.

Over the years, my passion for feet and how connected they are to the rest our body/mind/spirit led me to research many different modalities of healing. My research showed me that many cultures have dealt with foot care different ways.

As you will read in the next few chapters, what I have learned from my Western medical training has been supplemented by my immersion into Eastern Medicine as well as my fascination with what is frequently called quantum medicine. You will learn that the anatomy of the foot goes beyond bones and muscles and that in many ways the "sole" is connected to our "soul." Like the proverbial "Achilles Heel," the fact is that if you don't take care of your feet, your feet will cause problems in your body, mind, and soul. I do not want anyone to suffer if it can be avoided, and that is a big motivation behind *Whole Foot Revolution.* My passion to educate people about the importance of the feet, to be proactive when you go to the primary care doctor, to seek out specialists if you need them, and to do other wonderful things that will make your feet and mind feel good in a very revolutionary way. Believe me when I tell you, you are what you feet!

FOOT NOTES

Self Foot Inspection

Every morning when you come out of the shower, I would recommend that you sit in a chair and inspect each foot. I would look for any unusual openings or breaks in the skin, skin or nail discoloration, dark pigmented lesions, inflammation in the sides of the toe which can be indicative of an ingrown nail, or anything that looks suspicious and not normal.

It is imperative that diabetic patients do their foot inspections also at nighttime before they go to bed.

Get a small mirror that you can place on the ground and then put your foot above it to be able to see the bottoms of your feet. Many people are not able to inspect the bottoms of their feet as it is hard to see.

Chapter Two:

MIRRORS OF THE BODY

Eastern medicine is not about curing your
sickness. It's about keeping you well.
- Tim Daly

ENERGY HIGHWAYS

The feet are truly like a GPS system to help us navigate the entire
body. Every area on the soles of the feet reflect a body part, gland,
or organ. In acupuncture traditions, or Traditional Chinese
Medicine (also known as TCM), meridians that run from the
top of the head through the body and down each leg to the feet.
The three yang meridians that affect the stomach, bladder and
gall bladder and three yin meridians that affect the kidneys, liver
and spleen. Meridians are the pathways that TCM doctors use to
direct "chi" or life force into our organs and to various parts of
our body when they insert needles into the meridians to direct
healing energy into the afflicted area. Meridians run from the
top of the head to the feet and when there is a blockage–very

often caused by stress–the Chi becomes stagnated and slows down causing illnesses and diseases.

While *Whole Foot Revolution* is not specifically about acupuncture or energy healing, there is a wealth of evidence about TCM, as it has been a revered method of health and longevity for over 2500 years. While Western medicine is unparalleled for emergencies and traumas, its methods have been around for a few hundred years at the most–so from my perspective as a doctor–the wisdom of ancient practices to work with our body's own healing systems by unblocking stuck energy is a vastly important consideration if you want to stay young and healthy.

A good analogy of a meridian for those not practicing TCM is to think of a highway with cars moving in both directions. Driving on a free-flowing highway is a pleasant experience that gets us where we need to go much faster than meandering through side streets. In the body, when chi is flowing through the meridians, then health is generally good. When a car accident happens on the highway and traffic backs up, or when too many cars get on the road at the same time and traffic slows down, that is analogous to the chi in our body becoming stagnated. In today's world where many people sit for too many hours every day or eat foods that release toxins in the body, and don't do exercises that put the bare feet on the ground (like Tai Chi, Qigong, yoga, or methods that you'll learn in this book) then we often feel that "stuck" energy in the early stage as pain or headaches or fatigue. As time goes on, that stuck energy can develop into bigger problems such as serious illness or disease or depression. We need to get the chi moving smoothly so that it flows just like it when you cruise down the highway on a sunny day without much traffic!

Acupuncturists try to locate
the area of the meridian in
the body that is causing the
blockage of energy, so they
can release the blockage and
allow more flow to the organs.

Acupuncturists try to locate the area of the meridian in the body that is causing the blockage of energy, so they can release the blockage and allow more flow to the organs. Evidence of this can be found when a patient experiences a problem in the foot or in the leg and they simultaneously experience issues with digestion, circulation, and even the heart or brain. That is why foot massage is so important in many traditions including Traditional Chinese Medicine, reflexology and Osteopathic practices. Even applying simple pressure from your thumb and finger to the soles of your feet can help. Giving your feet the proper attention that you will learn in this book will improve your health in ways that you never imagined.

FOOT NOTES

Stress Relief

If your shoes are on right now, put the book down for a moment, take them off and also take off your socks.

Looking at your sole on the bottom of your foot, find your second toe and follow it down with your thumb until you are a little proximal to the ball of your foot (fat pad) and feel an indent.

Now take your thumb and press into this indent and hold it in place for 60 seconds. How do you feel? This should make you feel calm, relaxed, and stress-free. This is a simple trick you can use whenever you are stressed and need a little relaxation. Now try doing this with your toes.

How do you feel? Can you feel how pressure on your foot can relieve tension in other parts of your body? This is because energy gets stuck in our body.

We all have the innate ability to heal our own body, by moving stuck energy.

THE SECRET OF CHI

Western medical training does not teach us about acupuncture or meridians or energy healing, but I started doing research on Traditional Chinese Medicine (TCM) a number of years ago, and that began my journey into healing through the utilization of acupuncture points, meridians, and subtle-body energy called chi.

In a way, chi is the bioelectrical part of the nervous system (you will read more about bioelectrical energy in the next chapter), and blockages or disruptions of the nervous system have an impact on people by manifesting as various disorders, illness, and even cancer. Finding solutions to unblock the stagnant within our nervous system can help us heal more quickly.

Chi is a subtle form of electricity that is not measurable in Western Medicine, yet it is essential to a holistic understanding of physiology. Electrical blockages in the nervous system impact health because these blockages stop the chi from flowing. This is an idea most traditional Western medical doctors don't necessarily agree with. The concept of chi is not taught in most medical schools and Western science has yet to qualify that there is another circulatory system that would have blockages such as blood flow.

Because I understood that acupuncture has provided tangible results with some of my clients, I knew I needed to investigate this further. Additionally, I have a very curious nature and always want to be open to learning, I decided to attend the *Traditional Chinese Medicine World Organization: Building Bridges of Integrative Medicine Seminar* in October of 2016 where I met Grand Master Lu. I was fascinated by learning a whole new perspective to help my patients get better faster and to live healthier and happier lives. The invisible healing energy called chi began to make sense during that seminar—even with my limited knowledge—and I began to see a connection between the feet and how diseases and illnesses are caused from stagnation or blockage of chi. I still retained some skepticism regarding chi because it wasn't measurable, and I am a type of person who likes measurements, but my curiosity was peaked!

Grand Master Nan Lu is the founding director and president of the *Traditional Chinese Medicine World Foundation* which is the country's foremost educational organization for traditional Chinese medicine or TCM. I still remember the first time I met Grandmaster Lu. I was on my way into the lecture hall at the conference where Grand Master Lu was going to be speaking. I went in a little early as I was getting excited to hear him speak. As I walked in, I saw him in the back of the room. I remember he was wearing a long sleeve red polo shirt and black pants and he had a short crew cut and was a lot shorter in height than myself. I have to admit, I was a little intimidated by him at the way he looked and the energy he exuded as I started to approach him.

I then went up to him and introduced myself. I remember when I shook his hand there was an energy that is hard to explain that went through my hand and into my entire body. I never felt this feeling before while shaking someone's hand. I will remember the sensation for the rest of my life. He had such a calm voice and was such a joy and pleasure to speak with especially when he found out I was a foot specialist. He also has a humorous side to him. I remember he asked if I played football at the University of Michigan because I was such a big guy. I told him I didn't, but love watching their football team and wondered how he knew I went to University of Michigan. I then asked him, how did he know I was from Michigan, let alone went to college at the University of Michigan, and he smiled and pointed to me and said, "Your shirt never lies." And then I looked at my shirt and realized I was wearing my University of Michigan sweatshirt. We both laughed and smiled.

I do remember he also told me that it was nice to see a Western medicine doctor opening up his mind to Eastern medicine and traditional Chinese medicine healing. I told him that I want to learn all facets of healing to help people that are suffering with chronic diseases and illnesses and to give them hope and other alternatives to healing their mind, body, and soul. After all, the soles of our feet are the key to our body's soul and is the only part of our body that touches and connects with the ground and Mother Earth. Our feet are the secret to our health and wellness.

Grand Master Lu founded Ming Qigong, a form of internal martial arts or a method of healing that comes from meditative movement. He is lineage holder of ancient knowledge not found in many of today's text books. Master Lu has devoted his life to helping patients heal their bodies, as well as guiding his Qigong students to discover their own healing abilities through their *consciousness* by helping them recognize how thoughts affect the body. Master Lu holds a doctorate in traditional Chinese medicine from Hubei College of Traditional Medicine in China and is a clinical associate professor at State University of New York at Stony Brook.

Grandmaster Lu has published many books on traditional Chinese medicine, and his latest book *Digesting the Universe: A Revolutionary Framework for Healthy Metabolism Function* addresses the multi-dimensional aspects of today's chronic health issues. While speaking at the seminar, Grand Master Lu asked if there were any questions, and I rose my hand. I informed him that I was a foot specialist and was fascinated with a statement in his lecture that in traditional Chinese medicine the foot is the most important part of the whole entire body and it is what they call the "enlightened" part.

According to Master Lu the foot is the only part of our body that touches and is in contact with Mother Earth and therefore it is generally the source of energy transference. The Chinese refer to the bottom central portion of the ball of the foot between the 2nd and 3rd toes as "bubbling fountain." This is the entrance point of energy flow and electrons from the earth through the feet and into our body for healing energy. It is also referred to as the K1 acupoint or kidney 1 point and also is connected to the solar plexus. Yin is connected to the head while yang is connected to earth. In qigong healing, the bottoms of the feet are also where we imagine negative energy or illness departing from the body. Traditional Chinese Medicine refers to the feet as enlightenment. The Chinese also look at the feet as sacred and consider the feet as the center of one's wholeness and balance.

According to Master Lu the foot is the only part of our body that touches the Earth and therefore it is generally the source of energy transference.

REFLEXOLOGY

Over the last few decades we have seen more and more Chinese massage storefronts in major cities with reflexology on their menu. We see a lot of these stores that have advertised on their windows "reflexology and foot detox" packages to improve health and wellness. Many people that pass by these storefronts and see the advertising on the windows have no idea what exactly reflexology is and don't even know how it relates to the feet. However, many people have sworn how a weekly foot reflexology session has remarkably improved their health and lives.

Mary, one of my patients found herself laid over in an airport for three hours with a terrible migraine. She was on her way to a very important business meeting and the stress was overwhelming. She was desperate as the Advil she took did not get rid of her migraine. Then she passed a massage stall with a sign that read "Reflexology." She remembered I had once told her I was studying it, so she felt she would give it a try. She discovered that just by slowing down and allowing herself to feel her own body and catch her breath the migraine became less overwhelming. She felt more peaceful and the migraine miraculously disappeared. She told me the story when she seen me for her visit in the office and was very appreciative that I told her about reflexology and its benefits. But was it really a miracle, or is there a science behind reflexology?

Laura Norman Holistic Reflexology Foot Chart

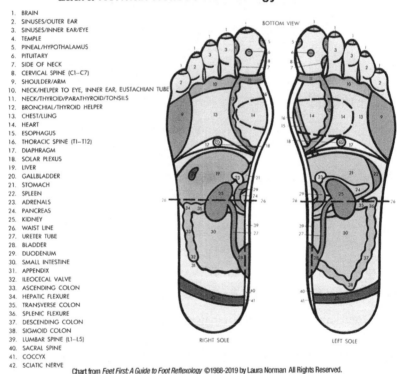

1. BRAIN
2. SINUSES/OUTER EAR
3. SINUSES/INNER EAR/EYE
4. TEMPLE
5. PINEAL/HYPOTHALAMUS
6. PITUITARY
7. SIDE OF NECK
8. CERVICAL SPINE (C1–C7)
9. SHOULDER/ARM
10. NECK/HELPER TO EYE, INNER EAR, EUSTACHIAN TUBE
11. NECK/THYROID/PARATHYROID/TONSILS
12. BRONCHIAL/THYROID HELPER
13. CHEST/LUNG
14. HEART
15. ESOPHAGUS
16. THORACIC SPINE (T1–T12)
17. DIAPHRAGM
18. SOLAR PLEXUS
19. LIVER
20. GALLBLADDER
21. STOMACH
22. SPLEEN
23. ADRENALS
24. PANCREAS
25. KIDNEY
26. WAIST LINE
27. URETER TUBE
28. BLADDER
29. DUODENUM
30. SMALL INTESTINE
31. APPENDIX
32. ILEOCECAL VALVE
33. ASCENDING COLON
34. HEPATIC FLEXURE
35. TRANSVERSE COLON
36. SPLENIC FLEXURE
37. DESCENDING COLON
38. SIGMOID COLON
39. LUMBAR SPINE (L1–L5)
40. SACRAL SPINE
41. COCCYX
42. SCIATIC NERVE

RIGHT SOLE   LEFT SOLE

Chart from *Feet First: A Guide to Foot Reflexology* ©1988-2019 by Laura Norman All Rights Reserved.

Reflexology as we know it today is based on an ancient form of therapy that focused on the hands and feet. A "reflex" is an involuntary response to a stimulus, and the word itself derives from the word "reflection." Like a mirror that reflects our image back to us, the specific reflex points of the feet mirror various parts of the body. While reflexology is not entirely the same as TCM from which the practice probably derived, it is still based on the same principles of holistic healing system that recognize the connection between the feet and the entire human system: body, mind, and spirit.

There is evidence of foot and hand therapy in China and Egypt as early as 2330 B.C. By 1600 AD the practice was used in Europe to alleviate various problems, from tooth pain to injuries in other areas of the body. By 1915, reflexology was known as "Zone Therapy" and was written about and practiced by doctors in Europe starting in the early 1900s.

Today, particularly in Asia, but also around the world in spas or reflexology centers, most reflexology foot massages begin with a footbath. The feet are soaked in a medicinal bath with up to 28 kinds of Chinese herbs. Then lotion or oil is massaged into the feet, ankles and calves. Following the laws of yin and yang, men's massages begin on the right foot and women's massage on the left. In many spas in the US, there is a trend towards "detox baths" for feet, in which a client soaks in a tub filled with minerals that attract toxins and pull them out through the feet. In just 15 minutes, the water becomes brown or even black depending on how many toxins the subject had in their body. You can find out more about foot detox products and other sources including the Whole Foot Revolution Wellness Store in the final chapter on Resources.

REFLEXOLOGY IN ACTION

In February of 2015, I traveled to South Florida to study foot reflexology with Laura Norman, one of the foremost teachers in the United States. I remember meeting Laura for the first time when I went to South Florida for reflexology training. She was so kind, pleasant, beautiful and welcomed me with open arms. She also had such a lovely training assistant, Sande, who was also so warm and inviting to me. I remember they both acknowledged me for wanting to learn reflexology and to be open minded to other healing modalities compared to other Western medicine doctors. They also stressed the importance of the soles of our feet and how important they are to our overall body wellness and how this would fit in perfectly with me being a foot specialist. It was obvious to me from day one that Laura had such a passion and love for reflexology and training others to learn all about it and its benefits to overall health and wellness.

Laura first discovered reflexology when she was a student at Boston University. She experimented with various mind and body holistic modalities as a student and found that reflexology seemed to have the most drastic and positive effect on her physically, emotionally, mentally, and spiritually. She then studied privately with many reflexologists in Boston and then decided to complete professional training and become a certified reflexologist. Laura started practicing in New York City and now also practices in South Florida. In addition, Laura also teaches and has certified training for those looking into becoming certified professional reflexologists.

It was highly informative as I appreciated her perspective on the eastern principle of chi. It was so amazing how I was able to connect the dots from what I learned from Grandmaster Lu

and Traditional Chinese Medicine and from what I learned from
Laura Norman and reflexology and how the feet are the secret to
health wellness of our mind, body, and spirit. It is also amazing
how our life energy or chi needs to be open and flow freely for
our body to be in balance and all the organs to work properly
in homeostasis. If we have a blockage we need to open it to be
healthy and prevent stagnation which causes our body to be out
of balance and for problems, illness, and diseases to occur.

Energy balancing and proper energy or chi flow throughout
our body from our head down to our feet is essential for us to
maintain our health and wellness. I have learned so much from

Grandmaster Lu's approach with Traditional Chinese Medicine and Laura's approach with reflexology as amazing healing modalities to us and our body as a "whole" as this "wholistic" approach to healing is what is missing in today's medicine. We as a society, need to look further into holistic and alternative ways of healing our bodies and understanding the true root cause of the diseases, illnesses, and chronic pain we suffer on a daily basis.

However, I have to admit, as a Western foot doctor I did have a bit of skepticism about the effectiveness of treating specific conditions through manipulation of the feet. Through my experiences both personally and with my patients, I am now a firm believer in the healing benefits.

By intentionally massaging the correct areas of the feet, we can stimulate over 14,000 nerve endings that help open the neural pathways throughout the body.

What I learned from Laura is that by using skillful application of the thumb hands and fingers to these reflex points, the body systems shift toward greater balance and homeostasis—body's natural ability to find equilibrium. Reflexology can reduce stress (the probable cause of so many illnesses in today's world), it relaxes the body and mind, improves nerve function, and helps in the body's detoxification process. By intentionally massaging the correct areas of the feet, we can stimulate over 14,000 nerve endings that help open the neural pathways throughout the body. Reflexology also improves vascular and lymph circulation that carries toxins out through the bloodstream and brings in oxygen and nutrients to our cells, keeping us more energized, more attentive, and strong. Simply pressing on the middle portion of the foot–at what we call the solar plexus area–people can relax and allow their bodies to de-stress and sleep soundly. By manipulating and adding pressure to the big toe on the bottom surface, reflexology seems to relieve migraine headaches. And the benefits extend beyond the body. The increased energy flow from foot reflexology also enhances our emotional well-being, which is very much why many people of all ages are flocking to yoga and meditation classes these days.

CONSOLING A BABY

On a flight back to Detroit after the reflexology workshop, I was sitting in front of a mother who was holding her baby boy. The child was crying and screaming, and the mom was unsuccessful in trying to console him. I took it upon myself to turn around and introduce myself to her and inform her that I am a foot doctor in Michigan and had just taken a course in foot reflexology. I asked if she would be open for me to show her a technique to hopefully help for her baby boy.

The baby boy was still agitated and crying as I spoke with her, but she agreed took his shoes and sock off. I told her to take her thumb and put it right on the mid-portion of the foot, right under the ball of the foot in the 2nd interspace between the 2nd and 3rd metatarsal bones. I instructed her to hold the point for about thirty seconds. I was teaching her to manipulate the solar plexus point of the foot, which is an important reflex point on the foot and great at relaxing and calming down the nervous system and body. The solar plexus is located in the chest area of our body slightly below the diaphragm and is a complex network of nerves in our autonomic nervous system that regulates the functions of our organs in our body. This reflex point (K1) is the key area on the bottom of our feet that allows us to relax, relieve stress, tension, and to be in a grounded state. After about 15 seconds, I noticed that the baby boy was calming down and not crying as much, and ultimately, he relaxed and fell asleep.

The mom was so appreciative that it really opened my eyes to how effective this simple but ancient modality was. I was a little amazed, because with any new approach I always want to experiment and test its efficacy. In this case, the proof was in the calm baby. The foot is truly the foundation to our body, and it is a mirror to the soul of our body. I needed to learn more about what they have known for thousands of years in the east, but I was on my way to knowing much more than I did when I graduated from medical school.

THE SOLE MIRRORS THE BODY

Reflexology recognizes five zones to the sole of the foot that mirrors the organs, glands, and parts of the body. The 5 zones of the foot are divided by 4 distinct horizontal division lines at the base of the toes, base of the ball of the foot, mid-arch area, and beginning of the heel area. These division lines are referred to as the neck/shoulder line, diaphragm line, waist line, and pelvic line respectfully. What is also interesting is that when we look at the inside or medial part of our foot where the arch is located, this is indicative of our spine in our body and our spinal reflex.

I find it so amazing and fascinating how the bottom soles of our feet mirror the exact location of our organs, glands, and parts in our body. For instance, the organs on the right side of the body are on the exact location on the bottom soles of our right foot and the organs on the left side of the body are on the bottom soles of our left foot in the exact location. In other words, each foot represents that particular half of the body. This is similar to a GPS that we use to find different places when we are driving. The focal reflex points on the soles of our feet are indicative and are a GPS to our entire body. For instance, if you had pain to the lower right region of your abdomen, when you pressed on the exact GPS location point on the bottom of the right foot, it would be painful. In other words, they are mirror images of one another. That is why there is so much that is brilliant about the connection between our feet and our body.

The bottom soles of our feet mirror the exact location of our organs, glands, and parts in our body.

As stated previously, there are 5 zones on the bottom soles of our foot going both horizontally and vertically. The zones going vertically are very easy as each zone corresponds to the respective toe and goes parallel up the body. For instance, the first zone is on the big toe and moves parallel down the foot and up the body. The second zone is on the 2nd toe and moves parallel down the foot and up the body, and the 3rd, 4th, and 5th zone following the same pattern.

The 5 horizontal zones on the sole of the foot which I described earlier are divided where the tip of our toes to their base correspond to the head and neck. The balls of our feet where our metatarsal bones are located and where our fat pad is located, correspond to our chest, lung, and heart. The upper part of the arch in our foot from the diaphragm line to waist line corresponds to our upper abdominal organs. The lower part of the arch in our foot from the waist line to the pelvic line corresponds to our lower abdominal organs. And the heel area of our foot corresponds to pelvic area organs. In addition, the heel area also corresponds to the sciatic nerve. The reflex point is like a stirrup running on both sides of the heel as well as the bottom of the heel. If you suffer with sciatica, this would be the perfect area to work on with reflexology.

Besides the 5 zones to the bottom of the foot which I described above, the ankle area corresponds to the reproductive organs in the pelvic area. In addition, the inner medial side of the foot corresponds to our spine including its curvature and the outer lateral side of the foot corresponds to our arm, shoulder, hip, leg, knee and lower back.

FOOT NOTES

Discovering Your Five Zones

Here is a fun exercise you can do now to find the five zones on your foot.

Take your shoes and socks off and bring your right foot up so you are able to see it and use your left hand and press down on it. Using your left thumb, press the tips and tufts of your toes until you reach the end of it. This is your head and neck zone area of our body.

Next, move your thumb farther down until you reach the hump at the ball of your foot. A plantar fat pad is located at the ball of our foot underneath our metatarsal bones and move your thumb from medial to lateral along the ball of your foot at the fat pad. This specific area corresponds to our chest, lung, and heart zone area of our body.

Next, continue down the medial side of your foot with your thumb until you get to the midway point of your arch of your foot. This entire area under the ball of the foot to the mid arch area corresponds to the upper abdomen zone area of your body.

Next continue moving down the bottom of your foot with your thumb from the middle of your arch until you get to the beginning of your heel. This entire area corresponds to the lower abdomen zone area of your body.

And lastly, continue down your foot with your thumb from the beginning of your heel to the end of your foot and this corresponds to the pelvic zone area of your body including your sciatic nerve.

You can now perform the same exercise on your left foot using the thumb of your right hand. Congratulations, you now know where the 5 zones to your feet are located.

OSTEOPATHY

Osteopathic medicine offers hands-on diagnosis and treatment through a system of treatment known as osteopathic manipulative medicine. Founded in the late 1800s by a medical doctor who recognized that many medical practices did more harm than good, he developed a system to help the body heal itself while still incorporating research and medicine that was helpful. Today, medical students in osteopathic medicine take the "Osteopathic Oath" to uphold and maintain the essential principles of the philosophy of osteopathic medicine.

The main principles of osteopathy focus on the notion that we are more than just a body, but rather we are body, mind and spirit. They believe that the human body has its own innate intelligence with the ability to self-regulate and therefore self-heal. They see the reciprocal relationship between the structure of the body and its functioning. Osteopaths base their treatment on this interrelationship of structure and function and to restore health through restoring self-regulating processes.

Contemporary Osteopaths practice an evidence-based medicine, and many medical practices, including the best university practices, now include Osteopaths on the staff. It is a branch of the medical profession in the United States and Osteopathic Doctors (D.O.s) are fully licensed physicians who practice medicine and surgery in all 50 states and are recognized in 65 other countries. The big difference between a DO and a general MD is that osteopathic medical students take 200 additional hours of training in the art of osteopathic manipulative medicine which is a system of hands-on techniques that alleviate pain, restores motion, support the body's natural healing functions and influences the body's structure to help it function more efficiently.

The osteopathic medical philosophy is akin to the tenets of holistic medicine–*suggestive of a kind of social movement within the field of medicine*–that promotes a patient-centered, holistic approach to medicine, and emphasizes the role of the primary care physician within the health care system. My hope is that through more education, osteopaths will influence a movement that recognizes the benefit of manipulation of the feet. Maybe one day the *Whole Foot Revolution* will influence more medical doctors to take natural healing approaches more seriously.

Reflexology is sort of like a mini morphine drip because it produces endorphins and when we are in pain, we want the endorphins to reduce our suffering. There are more and more studies now on how reflexology can reduce post-op pain, thus reducing the need for prolonged pain medication. Dr. Mehmet Oz is a proponent of alternative medicine. He has been a professor at the Department of Surgery at Columbia University since 2001, and he also directs the Cardiovascular Institute and Complementary Medicine Program at New York-Presbyterian Hospital. They have their own reflexology protocol for post-op pain that gets patients up and going quicker than traditional methods such as physical therapy.

There are many hospitals here in Michigan that are now getting their own holistic alternative treatment centers and some insurance companies now cover these kinds of services as they are seeing the cost benefits and the efficacy of patient results. I believe that physical therapy will eventually be replaced in the future with holistic alternative treatment modalities such as reflexology, medi-cupping, shiatsu, meditation, tui-na, and other alternative naturopathic holistic treatments. These "wholistic" treatment modalities will help to heal the "whole" self and body through the mind, body, and soul.

LEN BECOMES A BELIEVER

My cousin Len and I planned a special trip to Los Angeles, and we had tickets to be in the audience of the Ellen Degeneres Show. She is someone whom I truly admire, as she is such a loving, compassionate, and amazing human being who spreads love and positivity into this world.

Another reason we were going to Los Angles was to do my own random act of kindness. I had shipped 50 pairs of new shoes and socks to my friend Jared who lives in Hollywood. Len and I met up with Jared and his cameraman Jake and we hit the streets introducing ourselves to the many homeless folks camped out on the streets.

What an amazing day it was, but we were pretty exhausted and needed to catch our flight back to Detroit. As we were walking into the airport terminal, I saw Len was grimacing and looked like he was in pain. All of the walking we did in Los Angles, pounding the pavement of Hollywood had caught up with Len. He was having lower back pain as well as some sciatica pain shooting down his leg. As we were walking in the terminal we saw a spa that had a sign for reflexology. I was so excited and told my cousin that this is exactly what he needed. He really didn't know much about reflexology but trusted that I know something about foot massage considering my profession.

Still, Len walked into the Spa with much resistance and pain and walked out with no pain at all. I was so happy and felt great and my cousin was absolutely amazed and happy that his back pain and shooting pain from sciatica was completely gone. This is one of many personal experiences I have had with reflexology and the true benefits of healing through your soles. Try it out, and tell me what you think? You will be totally amazed at how you feel!

STRESS KILLS

Approximately 80% of diseases and chronic illnesses are caused from stress. Stress and anxiety create tension in the body. If we don't take the time out to address stress it could manifest into a plethora of conditions. The first sign of accumulating excess stress is tightness of muscles. Many time people that are suffering from stress and anxiety are sub-ventilating. Not bringing enough oxygen into the body will create a rigid posture and low energy.

Many time people that are suffering from stress and anxiety are sub-ventilating. Not bringing enough oxygen into the body will create a rigid posture and low energy.

Something as simple as reflexology can help with that and an overall anxiety stress.

Relieving stress on yourself or loved one is as easy as putting a little pressure with either your thumb or your finger on your feet. Even if you don't know the exact points, you could improve overall body wellness with foot massage. Just like there are stress balls that you can squeeze to release stress, you can get a foot massage roller and slip it under your desk at work. The ridges rolling across the sole of the foot will give you great relief. I use my own stress foot massage roller at work under my desk every day and it is so calming and therapeutic and also allows me to think clearly and have energy to be able to see all my patients throughout the day.

When a baby is stressed, they can become colicky. Here are a few simple tricks you can try to make your baby relaxed and can make a wonderful nighttime ritual for babies that are colicky, is to push and squeeze their feet starting from the toes and working down the feet. At the end of the session you can push your thumb into the middle of both feet at the area of the solar plexus for about 60 seconds which I discussed earlier in the book. This is very soothing for babies and will allow them to become relaxed and a lot of times go right to sleep and have a very restful sleep throughout the night.

CHRISTINA'S STRESS STORY

A young woman came into my office complaining of chronic pain to her feet and ankles. She also stated that she had some lower back pain and pain to her knees, especially with heavy activity. Upon speaking with her she mentioned that her mother was currently in the hospital and that her father recently passed away 3 months ago. She also informed me that her mom has been in and out of the hospital for the last month and has been doing a lot of running around between going to work and the hospital to see her mother, as well as balancing her family life and 2 young girls.

She told me that she has been struggling with so much stress lately. Her life was so busy, and she was neglecting her own self-care. During her evaluation it was noted that she had foot mis-alignment to both feet which was causing her chronic foot and ankle pain. I also explained to her that the stress she has been experiencing causes inflammation in the body and is also attrib-uting to her chronic foot and ankle pain. I educated her on some natural holistic modalities she can do at home to help with her stress. I educated her briefly on reflexology and gave her a few tips on some major reflex points she can work on when she goes home to help with her stress. I also recommended she do Epsom salt and water soaks along with adding lavender essential oil to the soaks to help soothe and calm her body through her soles.

I remember Christina was so amazed and fascinated at this infor-mation and best of all she was open to doing them. I made her some custom orthotics for her feet which are basically like glasses for the feet. The custom orthotics will help with the alignment of her feet as well as the entire body and the holistic modalities will help with the alignment of her mind and soul. I remember her coming back to see me in the office about one month later and she gave me a big hug and thanked me for getting her life back. She told me that she wore her custom orthotics daily as recom-mended and followed all the holistic tips I gave her to help with her stress.

She told me that her stress had been reduced substantially and that her chronic pain was almost completely gone. She was able to live a pain-free and active lifestyle with her husband and 2 girls. Most importantly, she told me that her mother was doing better and was back home and hasn't been back to the hospital. She also told me that her mom is doing daily soaks for 30 minutes with Epsom salt and water and adding lavender essential oil to the soaks. Moments like this are why I do what I do and why I love to help people through alternative holistic methods in the healing of their mind, body, and spirit.

FOOT NOTES

Healing Light Exercise

For the moment, become aware of your breathing. Is it deep or shallow? Let's do a little breathing exercise.

Close your eyes and take a deep breath and imagine a beam of bright white light coursing from the top of your head, moving throughout your body, all the way down to the tip of your toes in your feet.

Imagine you are transporting this healing and radiating energy down to your feet. With your exhale feel yourself releasing all the stress, tension, and negative energy from the tip of your toes all the way out through the top of your head.

Continue with the visualization and breathing exercises for at least another 5-10 minutes. How do you feel?

Headaches are so painful and miserable when we have them. Have you ever been at work or home and had an excruciating sharp pain on one or both sides of your head? A lot of times this pain can be localized to one particular area of your head or radiate and can sometimes feel like you have concrete cap on your head or like a vise around your head. The good-news is there is help and you don't need pills to help. There are some simple techniques you can do which I discuss below which will help rid you of your headaches.

I tell a lot of my patients about this simple approach in helping to treat their headaches. The best feeling is that when I see them for their next visit, they thank me that I helped them with their headaches and best of all they would spread their knowledge to help other friends, family, and co-workers.

FOOT NOTES

Healing A Headache

Have you ever suffered with
headaches that made you feel
absolutely miserable? Did you want
to look for your medications, but had
none to take or were not available
when you started having your
headache? Well I have the solution
for you by doing this simple exercise.
Best of all you do not need pills to
rid you of your headache pain.

If you are starting to get a
headache, I would recommend
that you take your shoes and socks
off first. Then take your thumb and
press in the middle of your big toe on
the same foot side as your headache
pain is located. Start to work the
reflex points on the big toe all around
it including the sides.

Then do the same technique to each
of the digits for approximately 1
minute per digit. If your headache

is located along both sides or the entire head area, I would do this technique to both feet.

In addition, I also have some of my patients use peppermint essential oil on the toes as they are performing reflexology using thumb and finger pressure in a milking fashion to each toe, concentrating mostly on the big toe.

Peppermint is a great essential oil you can rub on the soles of your feet to help with other pain areas in the body. In one of the later chapters of this book I will give you some tips and suggestions on some great essential oils you can use for various conditions or problems you may be suffering with on a daily basis.

Reflexology encourages the natural drainage of the lymph, the body system that carries waste products away from the tissues back toward the heart. After surgery, a lot of "garbage" material is released into the lymphatics and it comes out of the body, but reflexology and chi work help drain the lymphatics more quickly. On or more practical note, when you feel a cold or virus coming on, having a lymphatic massage will often unclog the build-up of toxins in the lymph and release them so that the body's natural defense system can do its job.

CRYSTAL'S STORY

Crystal, a soft-spoken young woman who had minimally invasive bunion surgery performed by me, came for her one-month post-op follow up appointment. She was feeling good and didn't have any major pain, but said she was having some difficulty getting her foot to fit in certain shoes because of the swelling.

She also told me that her best friend was getting married in 3 weeks and that she wanted to wear her dress shoes for the wedding. I told her about reflexology and its benefits for post-op swelling, healing, and recovery. She was open to having it done. After three reflexology sessions, Crystal was feeling great and her surgery post-op edema was decreased substantially. She brought in her dress shoes for the wedding and was so ecstatic that she could get her foot to fit into her shoe and able to walk without any major pain and no more bunion. She was so happy and grateful.

TYING IT TOGETHER

There is nothing better than getting your foot massaged, even with your loved one every night for fifteen minutes to half hour. You will feel more relaxed, and maybe even euphoric because massage helps release endorphins in our body, eases stress and anxiety, and helps you sleep better. And finding a reflexology center to be treated with herbs and treatments by a trained practitioner is great too. You will feel more recharged the next day!

I absolutely love how reflexology makes me feel both physically and mentally. With the stresses of everyday life and treating patients on a daily basis, I have reflexology performed on me each week to keep my body balanced, healthy, and energized. I would highly recommend you try getting a reflexology session performed on you at least once. Once you try it, you will be hooked on it and will see how truly beneficial it is to your mind, body, and spirit. Most importantly it will help keep your body balanced and in homeostasis for your overall health and wellness. After all, your feet are mini maps to your body and healing your body through the soles of your feet is the best natural kind of medicine today.

INSOMNIA

Insomnia seems to be a very common problem amongst many people where they have difficulty falling asleep or staying asleep. According to "*Medical News Today,*" insomnia is a sleep disorder that affects millions of people worldwide. It will cause people to be very sleepy during the daytime and sometimes fall asleep at work or even while driving in their car. It affects people both mentally and physically and causes anxiety and irritability. My wife and I had this problem for a long time until I was fortunate enough to learn holistic alternative treatment modalities to help alleviate this problem for both she and I.

According to the National Sleep Foundation, 30-40 percent of adults in America reported that they have had symptoms of insomnia within the last year, and 10-15 percent of adults in America claim to have chronic insomnia. The major problem with insomnia besides not allowing your body to get its proper rest it needs, is that it has been associated with a higher risk in the development of chronic diseases. Our bodies need to recharge at nighttime and it is essential for our bodies and our immune system to be able to get rest and sleep to prevent diseases and illnesses.

MICHAELENA SLEEPS

Michaelena was a young woman who came to my office for a painful mass to her right foot. We somehow got on the subject of her children and she also started talking about how she has so much difficulty sleeping. She said that she is always tired and exhausted and has no energy during the day especially with her children due to her insomnia. I then asked if she ever heard of reflexology or essential oils. She said she did but never used essential oils or reflexology. I then educated her on the Kidney 1 (K1) point and showed it to her, so she could do reflexology on herself by using her thumb and pressing the reflex point on her feet for a little bit before she goes to bed and after told her to apply lavender essential oil on the bottom soles of both feet. She was amazed and said she would be so happy if it worked. Approximately 1 week later, she called the office and told my staff to thank me for my suggestion of the essential oil and reflexology and that she is now able to sleep through the night and has so much more energy. It was such a great feeling to help her improve her quality of life.

FOOT NOTES

Rubbing to Sleep

I recommend it be a nighttime ritual to rub each other's feet before we go to bed. The soothing nature of touching each other's feet is very relaxing, therapeutic and even euphoric in nature. Most importantly it will allow both people have less stress and anxiety and thus help with decreasing incidences of diseases and illnesses caused from stress and its ill effects of chronic inflammation.

Doing this nighttime foot rub ritual will also allow you to sleep deeper and will provide more rest for your brain and body.

Chapter Three:

YOUR BIOELECTRIC BODY

Heaven is under our feet
as well as over our heads."
- Henry David Thoreau

CONNECTING BIO-ELECTRICITY TO BIOCHEMISTRY

When I came back from the *World Conference for the Traditional Chinese Medicine*, I was filled with questions about how the bioelectrical system fits into healing our body, mind, and spirit. Our biochemistry is based on an alkaline-acid balance. I thought about how a battery works. I wanted to connect the biochemical system with the bioelectrical system. I figured there must be more to investigate.

Bioelectricity, in a very general sense, is the study of electromagnetic forces on the human organism (Marino, 2018, p. 2). The word itself derives from two Greek roots: *bios* and *elektron*, loosely linking biology with electricity. The origin of the word dates to around 1600, during a time when physicians were seeking to understand whether there was a force that kept humans alive. Was it purely biological (the heart and brain driving the body) or was there an unseen energy (God or a soul or some other electrical force) keeping us animated and creatively functioning? This dispute between the two theories: *mechanism* (that we are purely mechanistic and not driven by an unseen force) and *vitalism* (that we are animated by a soul or chi or some electrical energy) began with Descartes, Bacon, and Newton and have not been resolved in any uniform way across cultures and different modalities.

Throughout the history of medicine, some form of bioelectricity has been studied at one time or another. As early as 1791, a European scientist named Galvani proved indisputably that under certain conditions, human tissue can produce electricity without any intervention from metallic contacts (Marini, p. 14). Around the same time a scientist named Du Bois-Raymond demonstrated that electricity could be measurably generated when stimulating a nerve. While this measurement wasn't *purely* electrical based on the reported voltage reading (see *Modern Bioelectricity* for the full scientific debate), the explanation for the electrical charge seemed to be in the polarized nerve membrane, meaning that the interior of the nerve had a different electrical "charge" than the exterior. After a great deal of debunking by Western scientists, bioelectricity began to solidify with the advent of the EEG and EKG machines that measure electrical impulses in the brain and heart respectively.

After a great deal of debunking by Western scientists, bioelectricity began to solidify with the advent of the EEG and EKG machines that measure electrical impulses in the brain and heart respectively.

Viewed theoretically, this is largely the same "life force" that Oriental medicine calls chi. In acupuncture, the insertion of metal needles into the body that creates a very small electrical current that is sometimes experienced as a shock that runs from the needle into the body.

As I introduced in the previous chapter, in traditional Chinese medicine meridians are invisible lines that run through the body from point to point. Being a Western trained physician, I was looking for measurable outcomes of utilizing this electrical energy in today's world of healing. I also wanted to try and make sense of how to heal with something that is invisible such as chi and meridians so understanding bioelectricity became increasingly important. As I researched the topic more deeply, I found some interesting literature and articles on healing the body through bioelectricity and the nervous system that really caught my attention.

FOOT NOTES

Bioelectricity Visualization

Sit in a comfortable chair in a nice quiet space and take your shoes and socks off. Place your feet on the ground and sit up with your spine straight and don't cross your legs.

Close your eyes and imagine with every breath you are transporting electrons into the cells. Now exhale and feel the bioelectricity flowing through your body like electrons flowing through a wire and feel the energy and charging power of your body. Feel the energy going to all your organs, glands, and each body part from your feet to your head.

Continue with this breathing exercise and visualization for at least 5 minutes. How do you feel? This is a great practice to do every day.

As mentioned in the section on meridians, I found substantial information showing how nervous system blockages cause diseases and how outcomes can be measured. I knew from medical school which nerves can be seen through voltage that is measurable in the nervous system—and so it made sense to me that the meridians could be viewed as similar to the nervous system and the bioelectrical part of our bodies seems similar to chi. I especially liked that we can measure and see what the problem is regarding illnesses and diseases and how important our nerves are in our bodies. I was fascinated to learn about bioelectricity from an Eastern perspective and one of my main teachers in that field is Tom Tam.

TOM TAM

Tom Tam is an amazing human being and whom I consider a miracle healer. Tom is a well-known writer and healer worldwide. Born in Tai Shan, China, he came to the United States in 1975. Since 1982 he has been practicing acupuncture, Tai Chi, and Qigong with great success. In 1994, he developed a new modality of healing called "Tong Ren" which has helped many people world-wide by applying principles of bioelectricity with other methods to balance the body in a "quantum" way.

As I have previously written, the meridians are like a GPS system that links to pathways between organs and glands—as the autonomic nervous system—to the brain. When I studied with Tam and learned his approach to quantum healing and bioelectricity, it turned on a light bulb for me and made a lot of sense regarding the potential for bioelectricity applied to the nervous system as a healing modality.

The meridians are like a GPS system that links to pathways between organs and glands– as the autonomic nervous system–to the brain.

I also learned how current Western medicine emphasizes *biochemistry* (drugs) and largely ignores the bioelectrical and/or nervous system which makes up the "whole" person. Having an open mind and wanting to understand an integrative approach to helping patients heal by incorporating aspects of traditional Chinese medicine, I also wanted to apply the world of quantum healing and bioelectricity. I am convinced that patients can heal at a much higher rate than they currently do, and it is all tied to our feet!

Tam was very excited to teach me what he knew and wanted to share his healing approaches. When I visited him in July of 2017, he took the time to explain how everything worked and it made total sense. While I was there, I watched patients who were healing of so many illnesses and diseases that other doctor said were incurable, including cancer. I wanted to learn more so that I could likewise help others that are suffering with diseases or illnesses that are difficult to treat.

According to Tam's perspective, we are like walking electrical lines. Our nervous system are the electrical lines and if there is a shortage or a block, it will eventually cause disease and illness. Tam considers himself to be a body electrician that wants to find where the shortage or the outage of the electrical line is so that he can repair the break and allow the electricity to flow properly without any resistance. In the bioelectric modality, when the electrical lines of our nervous system are flowing without blockages, we can naturally heal ourselves of diseases and illnesses.

When the electrical lines of our nervous system are flowing without blockages, we can naturally heal ourselves of diseases and illnesses.

CHUCK'S HEALING STORY

A friend of mine, Chuck Christian, played football for the University of Michigan from 1977-81 Rose Bowl. After being exposed to the coaching of Bo Schembechler for 4 years, he believed that he could do anything and felt invincible. Bo's motto was "Those who stay will be Champions" and Chuck carried that mindset throughout his life and it helped him become successful. Almost 3 years ago, he faced a foe far more intimidating than an Ohio State University (OSU) linebacker, and it was cancer. His beautiful wife, LaDonna, a nursing professor, noticed that he was getting up 8-10 times per night to go to the bathroom. She told him that he needed to go see his doctor. After numerous tests and biopsies, he was told that he had stage 4 prostate cancer which had already spread to his bones.

One doctor told him that he had 3 years to live and he fired him the next day. The team of doctors wanted him to have 6 rounds of Chemotherapy and 6-8 weeks of radiation.

Chuck then called Milt, one of his painting clients, who had told him about a healer who has been saving the lives of cancer patients for over 30 years. Milt took him to a cancer class in Quincy, Massachusetts the next day. He had no idea what to expect. Milt introduced him to Tom Tam the founder of the Tong Ren Healing System. The class consisted of about 60 cancer patients. He was amazed at how light hearted the class was. He was terrified, and they were laughing and joking.

Tom Tam was the ring leader with his jokes and stories. He was intrigued at how Tom directed the class as to which acupuncture points to tap on their acupuncture figurines. People were able to feel heat, tingles and relaxation. Tom also had multiple devices and machines that he had created. People shared the devices with each other throughout the class. After class, about 4 or 5 men came over to him. They hugged him and patted him on the back. They encouraged him and told him to not be afraid. They too had been given a death sentence from prostate cancer. Yet they were still alive 10 and 15 years later. That was a load off his mind.

The Tong Ren Healing actually works. He bought a small Tong Ren machine and wore it around his waist that night. He only got up 2 times to go to the bathroom. Then he noticed that his new normal was 2 times per night instead of 8-10. His PSA went down from 69 to 34. His doctor thought it was because of the hormone pills he had prescribed for him. He said, "No doc, I never opened the pills. It was the Tong Ren Treatments."

He agreed to do a round of chemotherapy a few weeks later. He even took his little Bo bobble head with him. He had a very positive attitude. After the nurse gave him the chemo, he was told to come back the next day for the shot to prevent side effects. Later that day he went to the gym to play basketball with the young fellas. He was terrible. He shot 0 for 8 from three-point land. He was ok with that. He was just glad to be able to play. The next day he began having trouble breathing.

The following day he could feel his body suffocating from the inside. He felt like he was naked, wrapped from head to toe with plastic wrap with a gorilla sitting on his chest. Each breath took so much work. He was afraid to go to sleep because he thought he would die. He was so helpless that when he tried to take out the trash, he couldn't do it. He was afraid to drive his car alone because he would get lost. He couldn't remember which side of the car the gas tank was on.

At 57 years old, he went from averaging 35 points per game in a 18 and over league. He was MVP and won the championship.

The following week after chemotherapy he couldn't walk to the mailbox. Now he knew why the doctor was giving him 3 years to live. The chemotherapy and radiation were going to kill him. The next day he went in to see Tom Tam sobbing like a baby. He gave him some special water that he made with one of his machines. He could feel the fear lifting and he was soon back to himself. He began making the special energy water for himself. He told his wife LaDonna that he had an interesting dream. He informed her that he wouldn't be doing anymore chemo or radiation.

Based on his dream, he knew that Tong Ren was the way to go. He had many people tell him how sorry they were that he had cancer. He always told them that if not for the cancer, he would never have found out about Tong Ren. And how he has used Tong Ren to help hundreds of people with all kinds of ailments. When he goes to the gym these days, he plays basketball for an hour and he does Tong Ren treatments for an hour. When he uses Tom's devices on knees, shoulders and backs, they are amazed. They usually laugh and say that the pain is gone in 5 or 10 minutes. They also try to convince him that the pain is gone. He calmly responds, "I know."

He sent a pair of Tong Ren glasses to his cousin Kenny. He is 70 years old and has been suffering from glaucoma and was almost completely blind. He also had leg pain that wake him up every 20 minutes. He taught him how to use the devices over the phone. After 3 days, he began seeing a difference in his eyesight and the leg pain no longer wakes him up. He called Chuck to let him know that he could see the numbers on his microwave. He said that this Tong Ren is amazing.

He had a client who was in her late 60's. She is a designer and has been suffering from severe pain in her replacement knee. The doctor set an appointment to replace the faulty knee with an updated version. He gave her a treatment before she went on a shopping trip to California. When she got back she informed him that she walked 3 miles a day for 5 days and her knee did not hurt at all. She called her doctor and canceled her surgery. She bought a Tong Ren machine and a few other devices so that she could do treatments on own. He had another female client in her early 70's who had a knee replacement done 4 years ago.

During surgery, she had an allergic reaction to one of the medications. It caused her to break out into blisters all over her vagina. Her doctors tried to clear it up for 4 years and nothing worked. Chuck got her a Tong Ren machine and told her how to use it. She could see improvements in 48 hours. I called her after a month and she was 100% cured. His wife, LaDonna was limping through the house one night. He asked her why she was limping. She had a big hump of arthritis on top of her foot. Her doctor wanted her to come in so he could cut it out. Chuck did a fifteen-minute treatment on her using his laser and Tong Ren knife. This was a no contact treatment. The bone hump went down 100% and the pain was gone. He repeated the treatment 5 weeks later and it never returned again.

Last year Tom Tam went to Italy to teach doctors how to use his Tong Ren devices. He also taught them about the blockage theory of healing disease. About 15 people traveled with Tom including Chuck. His wife sent him a text from Boston letting him know that she was having excruciating pain in her neck and shoulders. He did a long-distance treatment for her and 10 minutes later the pain was gone. There is no time or space/distance in Quantum Healing.

His oldest son Micah is the lead vocalist for the music group "Sons of Serendip." They were finalists on *America's Got Talent* 4 years ago. They are now traveling across the country performing for packed houses. They consist of a harp, cello, piano and vocals. They have a very unique sound. Chuck's son sent him a message that he was having trouble with his voice. His doctor said that his voice box was covered with nodules and could not sing or speak for 4 weeks. Tom sent him a Tong Ren machine and told him to wear it on his throat every night while he slept. After 3 weeks he went back to his doctor and the nodules were 100% gone. Two days later they had a concert and his voice was flawless.

His wife LaDonna developed a rotator cup problem in her right shoulder. She had surgery to correct the problem. Her rehab took about 8 months. She said that it was the most painful thing she had ever experienced. A year and a half later her left shoulder began to do the exact same thing. She began to cry because she didn't want to go through another shoulder operation. Chuck used the Tong Ren machine on her shoulder every night as she slept. Each day she would be out of pain until bedtime. After using the machine on her shoulder for 5 weeks the problem was gone. No surgery, no pain. She has been pain-free for 2 years. And if it ever comes back we know how to heal it.

One day he was in the gym watching a 6'7" specimen of an athlete playing basketball. It was a thing of beauty watching him play. That was until he came down on someone's foot and rolled his ankle. He screamed out in pain and actually cried a little. Chuck told him to hop over to his Tong Ren bucket and he would treat him. After using the laser and Tong Ren knife on him for 10 minutes, he could walk without limping. He said that 90% of the pain and swelling was gone.

Chuck went to a Michigan football game 2 years ago. He figured something must have bitten him, because his arm started to itch and swell. His hand blew up like a boxing glove. He ended up in the hospital for 4 days on antibiotics. Slowly his hand and arm began to go down. The doctor called it cellulitis. Three months later, the other arm began to do the same thing a small red patch the size of a coin began to itch like crazy. His wife told him to go to the emergency room right away before it swells up like the other one. He said no, because he wanted to see if the Tong Ren machine could take care of it. He wore the Tong Ren probe on his arm for 3 days and the itching, redness and swelling was 100% gone. His wife was amazed.

Chuck is also amazed at how many situations that he has been able to use his knowledge of Tong Ren and quantum healing. So many people are being helped. Tom Tam wants all people to have equal access to this technology. He is grateful to be able to call Tom a mentor and a friend. His ultimate goal is to change the world and save lives.

Similar to Chuck, I have so many amazing stories about healings of my patients, family, and friends through utilization of

Tong Rem and quantum healing taught to me by Tom Tam. I believe Tom Tam is a true miracle healer and I am so grateful and blessed that I have had the opportunity to meet and obtain so much knowledge about alternative healing modalities. Tom Tam possesses advanced knowledge that is way ahead of the times in healing and fortunately had the privilege of witnessing first hand.

BONES ARE LIKE BATTERIES

When we walk barefoot on the earth, the electrons from the ground and Mother Earth come up through our soles and because the bones are very highly insulated, the electrons actually become stored within the inner confines of our bones. Because all our bones are connected, electrons go in through our feet, through our legs and through the rest of our body.

Our bones are like batteries that store electrons.

In essence, our bones are like batteries that store electrons. During the course of the day, the bones store the electrons and in the evening time, they recharge all the cells within the body. In addition, as we get increased electron flow through our body from the ground, it also helps to neutralize free radicals in our body. Free radicals cause chronic inflammation, diseases, and illnesses. So, if we can charge our batteries on a daily basis similar to how we charge our cell phones then we can always be fully charged and decrease any type of illnesses or diseases for overall body wellness.

Our bodies function with both a biochemical as well as a bioelectrical function. Each of our cells are fueled by electrons which produce fuel by feeding the mitochondria and producing ATP. ATP is the source or the fuel that allows the cells to live and to function, like a battery in the cell. Bioelectrical energy is also part of the nervous system, and our nerves in our body all interrelate with the bioelectrical system.

If there is a blockage in the electric lines of the body, it is going to cause a problem not only with diseases, but also different illnesses and it is imperative to find where that blockage in the electric line is to heal the body and most importantly to heal the diseases.

In addition, the chemical makeup of the body involves the acid and alkaline levels in our body. A lot of issues and problems arise from having an acid environment within the confines of the cells and so that is why we want to try to balance out the acid in the body by having alkaline to neutralize the PH levels in our body. A good example will be with a car battery that has not only acid, but it also has electrical function. That is why if you have a dead battery, they always check the acid levels of the battery. Walking barefoot on the earth is a good way to restore acid/alkaline.

The rubber in the soles of our shoes acts as an insulator that blocks the proper flow of the electrons within the ground and up through our soles and into the bone.

The electrical function needs to have a source, or a spark plug to allow the electrical function to work, and if there is a blockage in the cable then it will not allow the battery to properly function. It also occurs with the acid levels of the battery. That is why in Western medicine, drugs and supplements and other chemical products might help with different diseases, however, they fail to address the bioelectrical function of the body. That is why it is estimated that 30% of diseases are able to be healed and there are 70% that are not able to be improved or healed.

The rubber in the soles of our shoes acts as an insulator that blocks the proper flow of the electrons within the ground and up through our soles and into the bone. If you are not getting as much electron flow or charging you can take your socks and your shoes off and just allow your feet to be barefoot on the earth. It is important to allow your feet to breathe and get oxygen just as our lungs need oxygen. Oxygen helps alleviate stress through our breath, and our feet also needs to alleviate stress and pressure from our shoes by walking on a daily basis. And as a side note, when walking barefoot make sure that the surface is not hot, as some people that have decreased sensation or neuropathy and can burn their feet.

In the case of diabetics that have neuropathy, you need to be careful not to step on any foreign objects on the ground that can cause a puncture wound within the bottom of the foot. Ultimately, when walking barefoot, you just want to make sure that you watch where you are walking and also make sure the surfaces are tolerable to your feet and no hazards as well. I always enjoy walking and grounding myself on the beach and especially the sand which can be very relaxing, but make sure that there is no shell or anything sharp that can puncture through the bottoms of your feet. As with anything, common sense is always important in keeping your feet safe and healthy. We need to honor our feet just like we do our head and we also need to focus on the health and care of our feet.

FOOT NOTES

Barefoot in the House

The first thing I do when I get home is I take my shoes and socks off and walk barefooted. The feeling of my feet on the floor is so relaxing and therapeutic.

I try and walk barefoot as much as I can as it is like having your own reflexology session on the bottom of your feet, and best of all its free.

I would suggest that you try this new simple habit daily when you get home by simply taking your shoes and socks off and walking around the house. It will feel a little strange at first, but your body and feet will eventually adjust and love you for doing it.

LOMAS HEALING STORY

My friend, Lomas Brown Jr., a former NFL Super Bowl Champion, and former offensive lineman for the Detroit Lions was experiencing chronic pain in his right foot and ankle. After playing college and then professional football in the NFL as an offensive tackle for 18 seasons, he suffered with a lot of wear and tear injuries throughout his body including his feet and ankles. I mentioned the various alternative healing modalities that I am performing to reduce chronic pain and inflammation. Lomas was very open to trying these alternative treatments and came to my office where I educated him about Traditional Chinese Medicine, bioelectricity, quantum and gravity wave healing.

He reported feeling better even at the first appointment, estimating that he was about 60% improved. I performed Tong Ren healing along with quantum gravity wave healing to remove blockages in the bioelectrical nervous system that was aggravating his chronic inflammation and pain in his right foot and ankle. I then had him come in for another treatment which helped him feel about 80% improvement. I told him I wanted to do one more treatment to try to get as close to 100% pain free as possible. I also evaluated his walking gait and foot biomechanics and noticed that both his feet were misaligned, so I did a digital-image-castings of both his feet to make custom orthotics devices. Custom orthotics help control foot misalignment and gait similar to how eye glasses correct vision. Shortly thereafter, I saw Lomas at a charity function and he thanked me for helping him and said he feels great and he raved about being pain-free. He has gotten back to an active lifestyle, has lost weight, and reports that his energy levels have improved substantially. He was so appreciative that his wife and entire family come to see me for their foot wellness!

TUI-NA

Tui Na is very popular as a means of healing in China and is starting to become more popular in the United States. Tui Na has been around in China even before acupuncture and has a very long history. In Chinese, the word Tui means "to push" and Na means "to grasp." In other words, Tui Na is the Chinese version of American massage that employs hand manipulation of different parts of the body for healing by separating and loosening tissue to open up blockages especially in the neck and shoulders.

My research into energy work lead me to Tui Na—an ancient form of Chinese bodywork that encompasses massage, acupressure, and body manipulation. By applying pressure to specific acupoints, meridians, and groups of muscles and nerves, blockages can be released. Tui Na harmonizes the yin and yang in the body through the manipulation of chi in the acupuncture channels—particularly in the neck where the vagus nerve is found—restoring balance in the body that leads to improved health and vitality.

Unblocking the arteries and nerves in the neck is important because it supplies blood and oxygen to the brain. The vagus and phrenic nerves link to the brain, and when the nerve is blocked the "bio-signals" or chemical messages are likewise blocked. This blockage depletes our hormones and other biochemicals in the brain and causes stress to our nervous system and organs. Many people in our modern culture put excessive stress on the neck through working on computers and phones all day and most massage therapists will tell you how stiff most people's necks are! Tui Na goes beyond relieving a sore neck by helping unblock the pathways in the body.

THE VAGUS NERVE

Building on the craniosacral theories of various scientists, including Stephen Porges's *Polyvagal Theory*—considered one of the most important developments in human neurobiology—the connection between many symptoms including anxiety, depression, migraines, and back pain are linked to a blocked vagus nerve. Porges's work also explores the link between a well-regulated vagus nerve and social functioning. His findings and methods offer hope that by working with the vagus nerve we might improve social behavior, making it possible to alleviate some of the symptoms at the core of many cases of autism spectrum disorders (*Accessing the Healing Power of the Vagus Nerve: Self-Help Exercises for Anxiety, Depression, Trauma, and Autism, p. 3*).

The soles of the feet have the corresponding connections to the neck from the base of each of the toes at both feet. By stimulating these areas, individuals who have stiff necks or perhaps vagus nerve blockage resulting in pain or migraines can find a lot of relief, particularly if the area is massaged daily. Likewise, working with the vagus nerve can help solve issues in the feet.

BIO-ELECTRICITY AND HEALING

Many patients are treated with prescriptions that cover the symptoms, but the conditions are not necessarily improving with current Western medicine. In 2014, *Newsweek* printed an article called *Mapping the Body's Wiring for Medical Breakthrough* giving credence to theories on bioelectricity that had been previously viewed as pseudoscience. That the *US National Institute of Health* is launching an effort to map the body's electrical wiring offers great potential for this healing modality. Since the article was printed, over $100 million has been invested into the development of electro-ceutical research.

Many medical doctors still do not believe in energy healing and therefore their knowledge is limited to biochemical and biomechanical processes. It is shocking that so little information about bioelectricity is available in the US today although it is a hugely researched topic in China because the entire history of TCM is based on energy and the electrical nature of the body. Remember that China's history of healing dates back thousands of years, while the US is only a few hundred years old. We still have much to learn!

Bioelectricity was discovered by an Italian doctor named Luigi Galvani in the late 1700s. The electrical charge in the human body can be tested with a simple voltmeter to test where blockages exist, and one approach to working with that blocked energy is what Tom Tam calls the Bioelectric Bypass Method.

Without bio signals from the nervous system, the hormone system cannot function properly.

Bioelectricity in the human body is complex. In very simple terms, without bio signals from the nervous system, the hormone system cannot function properly. Without hormones, our bodies cannot function. Bioelectricity is a way that the body communicates with all the complex systems.

There are several types of electrical fields in the Universe. One is the field created by nature. The earth has an electromagnetic field. We have learned to harvest electricity to power batteries to power lights, heat and cars. Electricity can come from the sun and also from radio waves. In the human body, each cell carries electricity. Our heart and brain's electricity can be measured with EKG and EEG machines. Many high school students have measured electricity coming off potatoes using a voltage meter which is a simple way of demonstrating electricity in living things.

The human body contains a type of electricity called bioelectricity that tends to be more acid or alkaline depending one's state of health.

Autoimmune disease is a state in which the body's natural immune system starts to attack its own healthy organs such as the liver, pancreas, spleen, stomach, and colon. It is important to have an acid and alkaline balance in the body to facilitate the body's homeostasis or natural healing ability. We don't want too much of an acidic environment in the cell as that will decrease the oxygen and cause diseases–particularly cancer cells from forming. It is essential for healing the body by making sure the acid alkaline levels of the cells are within a balanced state. Many foods such as processed foods, sugar and many carbs cause acid in the body, while vegetables and fruits (including lemons) create alkaline.

One theory for healing cancer came from Dr. Otto Warburg who won the 1932 Noble Prize for his discovery that cancer cells only thrive in highly acidic cell environments. Acidy builds up in the body from eating the wrong foods, and also from stress. Acidic cells thrive in low levels of oxygen. In addition, scientists discovered that the body's low bioelectricity also cause cancer cells. It makes sense to balance your diet to reduce acidity, and also helps your immunity to increase piezoelectricity.

Acidic cells thrive in low levels of oxygen.

For instance, patients who have multiple sclerosis usually see a neurologist for treatment, but really, MS is an *autoimmune issue* because when MS is taking over our body, it is because our T-cells are out of control and are destroying portions of the normal nerve pathways. The nerves are what innervate the arterial flow in the arteries, and when there is a blockage, the decreased circulation will cause a lack of oxygen. Lack of oxygen produces a lot of problems, not only with the acid-base component of homeostasis in the body, but also with the cells, nerves and other organs.

FOOT NOTES

Oxygentating Your Cells

Here is a good deep breathing exercise you can do at home to help bring oxygen and life into your cells of your body.

Sit in a comfortable chair and breathe deeply in and visualize blue light enriched with energy source and oxygen coming into your body through your nose and body.

Visualize this blue light flowing throughout your entire body from your head all the way down to the tips of your toes nourishing and providing oxygen to all the cells of your body.

Then let the air out of your body and visualize red light leaving your body from the tip of your toes exiting out your mouth and nose with all the toxins and impurities from the cells of your body.

Continue this deep breathing exercise for a total of 10 minutes to help oxygenate and enrich all the cells of your body. How do you feel?

Our brain health relies on blood circulation. 20 to 25% of our blood goes to the brain, and the brain receives more blood flow or circulation than any other part the body.

What is even more interesting is that that brain is a very small percentage of our body—roughly 2% of our entire body—and yet it gets most of our blood. Back to the vagus nerve, a lot of people with disease and illnesses might benefit from unblocking the nerves that flow because our brains need that blood flow!

PIEZOELECTRICITY

Piezoelectricity is the electrical charge that accumulates in solid materials such as crystals and biological matter–like bone, DNA and various proteins–in response to applied mechanical stress. The first piezoelectric device in modern times is the sonar used by the military.

The electricity in the body is called piezoelectricity. In the late 1800s, Dr. Julius Wolff found that bone reshapes in response to the force of piezoelectricity. In the late 50s a Japanese doctor named Yasuda discovered that piezoelectricity could be measure as high as 300mV from the tibia when a subject was walking. We now know that piezoelectricity is required to stimulate bone growth, so applying electricity to a fractured or broken bone is now an approach used by healers (called "capacitative coupling"). Bones need calcium, Vitamin D, *and* piezoelectricity to heal. Just taking calcium alone will not help strengthen the bones and might even hurt the system by causing other problems such as gout which manifests as a very painful big toe. From a TCM perspective, many bone marrow and blood disorders are effectively treated by stimulating the T1 point to generate piezoelectricity within that meridian.

The ultrasound machine is one way that piezoelectricity is applied to diagnosis and to healing. A common machine that many healers use today is a TENS machine that focuses bioelectric energy into a damaged body part to accelerate healing and block pain without the use of prescription painkillers.

Many people confuse the electromotive force or EMF with electromagnetic force EM which has caused confusion about which type of energy we should embrace, and which type we should protect ourselves from. piezoelectricity is healing and should be embraced!

In TCM, the K1 point is the energy point for the yin meridian. This point is used to ground the energy in the body, and it is also useful for insomnia, nausea and even headache. In addition, we can also use this K1 point to charge the body's piezoelectricity by means of the electrons. According to traditional Chinese medicine theory, the kidney function controls the bone growth and the K1 is used to charge the energy or Chi in the entire body.

The K1 is located on the bottom of the foot, and the foot carries the whole body's weight. As we know from physics, the more weight that we carry, the more pressure is exerted. So, the soles of the feet produce more piezoelectricity than any other place within our bodies. Since all the bones in the body are connected, when we "charge" or activate the K1 point, the piezoelectricity will run to all the bones within the body. The soles of the feet and the K1 point are essential to charging our body's energy and thus promoting healing to our entire body. I encourage all my patients to take off their shoes and socks and walk in the **grass, sidewalk, sand, or dirt** as often as possible. This is really the heart of the *Whole Foot Revolution*! It will make your bones stronger, your heart healthier and your mind much more joyful. But it doesn't work unless you do it.

Chapter Four:

GROUNDING - THE EARTH BENEATH OUR FEET

The foot feels the foot when it feels the ground.
- Buddha

It is amazing how something as simple as taking off your shoes and socks and walking barefoot can change your entire life. Walking outside and becoming one with Mother Earth is something that our not so distant ancestors did far more frequently than we do today. The earth is filled with electrical charge that is beneficial to our health, but very often we aren't accessing this natural energy. Our modern lifestyle is filled with rubber which blocks the connection with the electrical charge of the earth. We wear rubber-soled shoes, drive cars with rubber tires, sleep on beds that are a distance from the floor and are also often in high rise buildings, and we work all day indoors at desk jobs. Grounding or "earthing" is a theory that out bodies can absorb energy from the earth with many benefits that range from physical to emotional. The Grounding Movement is a trend based on common sense backed up by scientific research that helps us correct the electrical charge in our bodies so that we can live healthier lives.

Michael Sandler, a Boulder, Colorado grounding expert points to multiple scientific studies including research by the University of California Developmental and Cell Biology at Irvine (2012) suggesting that our lifestyle has separated us from the vast supply of electrons on the surface of the earth resulting in physiological changes and stress. Sandler notes that humans become positively charged when we are not connected to the earth. We even accumulate a buildup of the positive charge from the air around us because of all the electrical equipment we use and that surrounds us passively even when we aren't using it. Most of us feel some strain or stress from working with electronics all day, including cell phones to computers. A lot of people–including an alarming rate of children–are on their cell phones from the moment they wake in the morning until they go to sleep at night, and most often leave their cell phones on and near their beds while sleeping.

In Sandler's workshops, participants are plugged into a grounding wire and placed beneath their chair. This wire grounds them to the earth to show them how it feels. Sandler also applies a grounding patch in an area of a participant's body that is in pain and about thirty minutes later, the pain and inflammation is significantly reduced. The implications for this work are huge. Rather than immediately downing drugs for pain, wouldn't it be great to sit or stand in the park with your feet in the cool grass? Of course, sometimes drugs are helpful to us, but sometimes they are truly unnecessary and ineffective.

I remember being stressed a few years ago which resulted in many restless nights and exhausting days. My energy was very low, and I was feeling a little bit down emotionally. Then I heard about "grounding" and it caught my attention. The science and the simple common sense behind this approach appealed to me tremendously, so I tried it out. I simply took my shoes and socks off and walked barefoot around my backyard for about 20 minutes, leaving my cell phone inside. As my feet touched the grass, the cool energy was like no other feeling I have ever felt.

At first, I felt a little tingly sensation that started in my feet and then ran up my body. As I closed my eyes and concentrated on the feeling I started to feel very happy. I felt as if I was becoming one with Mother Earth. I felt the earth literally holding me and absorbing my negative energy. I felt this was a real phenomenon and not my imagination, so I have continued to experiment with the practice and have guided many of my patients to do likewise, most of whom report extraordinary results.

During much of the year–weather permitting–I do this same grounding routine when I get home from work or in the morning before I leave for the office. Since starting this routine, I have increased my energy levels, decreased my anxiety and stress, and it has allowed me to sleep soundly at night which allows my body to recharge so that I wake fully energized in the morning. My grounding practice has also allowed me to lose weight without much effort and feel so much healthier all around.

And in our society where we are so insulated from the earth, I recommend doing this practice every day for at least 21 days and you will see how you change. I would even suggest to those that are sedentary and unable to walk here is an exercise you can do.

FOOT NOTES

Grounding Your Self

Get a chair and sit outside so that your feet are on the grass, sidewalk, sand, or dirt. Now just move your feet back and forth and enjoy the texture and how it feels and close your eyes visualizing that you are physically walking, and the healing energy is coming in through the soles of your feet.

 If for some reason you are not able to go outside due to the weather, there are various grounding devices that you can use such as grounding mats, grounding patches, and other grounding devices that plug right into grounding plug of your electrical outlet inside your home.

Be sure to share all your amazing stories with us online so we can share the benefits of the Whole Foot Revolution.

You can simply take your shoes and socks off and tune out of your busy world while listening to our 10 minute "walking meditation" audio which you can find in our store on our website at www. wholefootrevolution.com

A POWERFUL ANTIOXIDANT

When we walk with our feet directly on the ground without socks or shoes as a barrier we come into direct contact with the earth as our ancestors did for thousands of years. Some people might not identify with the idea of "Mother Earth" but for those who do, the energy that fills our body is nothing short of the love that a mother gives her baby. For those who prefer a more scientific explanation, it turns out there is more to grounding than taking time to feel a good sensation. Walking barefoot directly on the earth helps recharge our cells and neutralize free radicals. Free radicals are cells that lose electrons and become positive ions that are highly unstable and produce inflammation in the body. Putting the soles of our feet directly on the ground without socks or shoes acts as a method to neutralize free radicals. How? Electrons flow from the earth through the soles of our feet. Walking barefoot on the earth allows us to absorb large numbers of electrons, which bind with the free radicals and thus gives us more energy and available oxygen.

In the revolutionary book, *Earthing* (2nd edition: Basic Health Publications, Inc., 2014), Clint Ober, Stephen Sinatra, and Martin Zucker discuss in great detail the specific mechanisms and processes involved and the large body of scientific studies conducted by medical and physics researchers supporting the validity of earthing as a means for reducing inflammation and improving health.

The earth is thus negatively charged, and when we walk barefoot on the earth we absorb ions through the soles of our feet.

Approximately 65 miles above the earth's surface is a part of the atmosphere called the ionosphere which contains both positive and negative charges. Negative charges are transferred to the earth, usually by lightning storms which occur in excess at the equator. The earth is thus negatively charged, and when we walk barefoot on the earth we absorb ions through the soles of our feet. These ions assist the bioelectric system in our body to flow freely and replenish the cells in our organs, our heart, our lungs, our brain, and throughout our body. Grounding also helps to normalize our stress hormones by making oxygen more available to the body. As most of us know, stress is a huge contributing factor with disease and illness, and that is why we are often encouraged to breathe deeply to reduce stress. If we decrease our stress, we can improve our overall health and wellness. Grounding is the most potent antioxidant and de-stressor known to mankind.

This grounding process of walking barefoot is a natural way to balance our bodies through the soles of our feet. Walking barefoot is also like applying reflexology to all the pressure points on the bottoms of our feet as we explored in Chapter 2. When we walk on the ground without shoes, we flex our toes and numerous reflex points are naturally massaged. When we wear shoes that have rubber soles (and many women wear high shoes which basically isolate and remove any type of contact with earth) our feet stop exercising and the connection between the points in our feet and our organs and body parts is lost. Walking barefoot for even twenty minutes a day can counteract the negative effects of wearing shoes for endless hours every day and night.

Walking barefoot for even twenty minutes a day can counteract the negative effects of wearing shoes for endless hours every day and night.

As stated earlier, inflammation in our bodies produces an overproduction of positive ions in our body which we call free radicals. Free radicals are not good for our overall health and wellness and the nice thing with grounding our bodies and walking barefoot is that it allows us to alleviate inflammation by walking barefoot and allowing the electrons from the earth to come into the body through our soles and this is an important health discovery since we know that inflammation is a root cause of most diseases.

GROUNDED ENERGY

As mentioned earlier, the bones in our body are like batteries that get charged with electrons as we contact the ground barefooted. Many have become accustomed to using caffeine or sugar to energize our depleted bodies, but both caffeine and sugar will make our energy crash when the initial high wears off. Taking off our shoes and absorbing electrons would be more effective and would protect us in many ways beyond having a momentary sugar high. As we connect with the earth we are also allowing our body to find its natural state of homeostasis, or balance, along with an increase in electrons to minimize free radicals and inflammation.

Most of us have isolated ourselves from the earth in many ways that we consider "modern progress" such as having shoes and electronics. Now I'm not suggesting that we give up our shoes permanently, but to regain our balance in this world, and maybe even our sanity, we need to connect with nature so that nature can heal us. So many people are not one with nature nor do they appreciate the deep healing qualities and benefits of Mother Earth.

About 95% of people walk insulated on the earth—and some rarely walk at all—causing an increase in inflammatory related diseases and illnesses. As a physician, I am always fascinated by the root causes of illnesses and why many people do not heal very quickly and why some never heal at all. A lot of my patients complain of chronic, seemingly unsolvable problems even after visiting many doctors. They have a grocery list of medications that often cause other problems like a chain reaction. There is growing evidence by scientists and physicists that by utilizing grounding techniques patients suffering with chronic pain can improve when their feet connect with the earth.

GROUNDING THE PAIN

As we are aware many diseases and illnesses are caused from stress and inflammation within our body. Our feet are the secret to better health. The main silent killer today is inflammation, and we need to address it and rid it naturally through grounding. Many patients go to doctors including my specialty of treating feet, to treat pain that is secondary to chronic inflammation. I see a lot of patients with plantar fasciitis and also osteoarthritis which are secondary to Inflammation. Although I often treat these patients through a variety of Western medical approaches including injections, stretching, therapy, custom orthotics, and sometimes surgery, my preference would be that everyone took care of their feet better and grounded themselves, in which case other interventions would likely be unnecessary.

I often have my patients take their shoes and socks off and either stand or walk barefooted on the grass or ground for about 10-15 minutes daily. Many of the patients come back to my office and are so happy and say their heel pain from plantar fasciitis and their joint pain from the arthritis has improved and are pain free. I also had a personal experience where I was playing basketball with my son in the summertime and I went for a rebound and came down on my son's foot and twisted my right ankle. I was in a lot of pain and was hobbling around. I then took my shoes and socks off and sat on the grass with my feet (and my hands in this case) touching the ground while I was watching my son shoot the basketball since I couldn't play. After about 10 minutes I got up and was amazed that the swelling and pain was gone, so I finished the game with my son.

The science made sense, and my intuition tells me that the earth can help us heal faster. When we have an injury such as a bruise or sprain, the trauma damages the cell and the white blood cells will surround and encapsulate the dead or damaged area. It will then release a reactive oxygen that takes electrons out of the damaged cell and destroys the damaged cell. If there are enough free electrons to reduce the remaining free radicals (which are the positive ions) then they take the electrons from the healthy cell and damage it and the message to the immune system, then goes out and then another neutrophil comes in and then we will have a repeated chain reaction.

Anyone with chronic inflammation and pain with utilization of grounding will stop the oxidation process and decrease the inflamed portion and it will stop immediately. When inflammation decreases the body will heal itself naturally and return to normal. The healing of human beings will increase substantially with utilization of grounding because when the body is grounded then we can't have the inflammation. There are now over 20 published studies in peer reviewed medical literature that indicate measurable and repeatable positive effects from grounding.

Because inflammation is the root cause of many diseases and illnesses it makes sense that we will all be healthier if we can fit in grounding on a daily basis for as little as 10-15 minutes a day. There are now grounding mats and other grounding products that people can purchase if they are not able to go outside and ground themselves due to snow and cold weather. With rising costs of medical interventions for diseases, and the inconvenience and emotional drain that disease takes on individuals, natural cures are harmless, inexpensive, and they work. So why not try it?

When you think of it a typical day for any person is you wake up and get out of bed which is ungrounded and then you walk on the floor which is insulated from the earth and then we put our shoes on which is also insulated from Mother Earth. Throughout the entire day the majority of us are completely ungrounded and disconnected from Mother Earth. That's why when we go on vacation to a nice beach and we walk barefoot we are in a great mood and often don't notice any pain. In today's society, natural ideas are sometimes rejected, and we are brainwashed by science and pharmaceutical companies due to our current medical philosophy and their training. The greatest thing about grounding is that you don't need to have a doctor prescribe it to you, and best of all it's free without any risk of complications. The secret to healing is the earth and grounding yourself. This is a very special gift that was given to us from the earth itself, and we should accept it and living a healthy pain-free and active lifestyle.

MY GROUNDING STORY

For a long time, I have had difficulty sleeping at night when I went to bed.

I would wake up each morning feeling very lethargic with no energy and brain fog and a lot of times had pain in my neck with headaches. It was hard to concentrate and get through each day and I had very low energy levels. My mind and body felt absolutely miserable each and every day. I then learned about earthing and grounding mattress pads and sheets you can put on your bed to help ground yourself and re-energize your body as you sleep. I wanted to try them out and see how it worked for me as I was desperate to try anything.

I then purchased the bed mattress pad cover and grounding sheets. I put them on my bed and plugged them into the grounding outlet in the electrical plug in the wall next to my bed. I was absolutely amazed at how great they worked for me. I was able to sleep through the night soundly and actually able to remember my dreams which I was not able to do for a long time. The best thing was that I felt very energized in the morning and was very alert with a clear mind. I was not sleepy and had no brain fog, neck pain, or headaches. I now sleep every night with my grounded bed mattress pad and grounded sheets and feel so amazing when I wake up the next morning.

The most interesting part of it all is that my wife, who was also having very similar issues as I was with insomnia, decreased energy levels, brain fog and pain, told me that she was also feeling great. That's when I knew that grounding was for real and that it really works. I am a very skeptical person and couldn't believe how fast it worked in grounding my body and putting my body in homeostasis overnight. I have also told many of my patients about these grounding bed sheets and mattress pads and majority of them that have used them would come back to me when I would see them in the office and thanked me for giving them their life back. It is the best feeling to be able to help someone and give suggestions on holistic and alternative remedies they can use which will help improve their quality of life. After all, that is why I became a doctor in the first place.

My goal is to educate my patients and have them spread the word to their family and friends to help a lot more people. I am so grateful and blessed to have learned about these grounding bed pads and sheets and the positive impact it has provided my wife and me in healing our mind, body, and spirit. Grounding and rebalancing our bodies is essential to gaining our health, wellness and most importantly in allowing everyone to get their life back.

FINAL THOUGHTS ON GROUNDING

My dream is to encourage grounding as a normal routine for people who work in offices every day as a substitute for smoke or junk food breaks. I can imagine companies with courtyards with grass specially planted for employees so that they can put the soles of their feet on the ground and walk for fifteen minutes. These grounding breaks would allow more work productivity, less stress, more energy, and a lot more of a happier working environment. Being saturated by so much electronic energy causes our body's cortisol levels to increase at an alarming rate. Our brains are basically short circuiting, resulting in obesity, lack of sleep, and general stress. I hope that *Whole Foot Revolution* will start a trend towards grounding breaks in offices and business around the world!

FOOT NOTES

Lunch Break Grounding

Here is a great exercise you can do at work on your next lunch break.

Invite your co-workers to eat lunch with you barefoot in a nearby park or in a grassy area outside the building. You can make it a daily ritual and call it your "grounding break" instead of your lunch break. You can bring your bagged lunches and bring a blanket and put it on the ground.

Then have everyone take off their shoes and socks and put them directly on the grass while you sit.

Allow the earth's energy to flow through your soles into your body as you eat and talk with each other. Allow your feet to breath and feel free. When you are done eating your lunch you can then put your shoes and socks back on and start heading back to work.

Connecting with your co-workers:

On your way back in the office, check in with them and ask these questions:

How do you feel?

Do you feel more energized, clear minded, happy, and ready to get back to a productive day at work?

I can envision in the future that a lot of businesses will have mandatory grounding breaks for their employees to help with overall morale, happiness, and work production. But most of all the health benefits for its employees will be a lot better than providing a "smoke break" like many companies now do with their employees. Recharging our bodies by grounding ourselves on a daily basis is essential for overall health and wellness especially of our mind, body, and soul. That's why I feel recharging our bodies with "grounding breaks" at work will be seen a lot more in companies with their employees compared to the "smoking breaks" we are all used to seeing. We need to start encouraging more health outreach awareness in the working environment amongst employees and many companies will see the positive and win-win effects this will produce when implemented.

Chapter Five
QUANTUM APPROACHES

Cancer didn't bring me to my knees,
it brought me to my feet.
- Michael Douglas

GRAVITY AND HEALING

My eyes opened wide to a revolutionary theory of healing when
I attended the 2017 *Energy Healing Symposium* with Tom Tam.
Among many interesting topics, he presented a lecture on "gravity
medicine." Gravity healing considers the effect of gravity on the
body based on various scientific studies–primarily conducted by
NASA–that we will cover later in this chapter. While the NASA
research studies the effect of gravity on cell structure and DNA,
Tam has been exploring the field since 2011–a few years before
the scientific studies were published–from a hands-on perspective with his patients. Tam's general idea is that a "synchronizing
effect" (2018, p. 40) creates an energy of vibration from a device

called a "transducer" that is placed on a specific part of the body, creating a gravity field on that area.

According to Tam, gravity decreases in cells because of low bio-electricity, so when a cell loses one electron, it loses forty times its gravity. If we can charge a cell with a graviton or transducer, the cell will regain its density by taking on a new electron. Tam's work implies that the transducer can change the frequency of vibration in cells, thus removing energy blockages in meridians and in the nervous system. Tam's work focuses primarily on tumors of his patients, and while he even notes in his work on gravity healing that many reading his book will be skeptical, he reports a lot of success with this method.

Gravity healing from NASA's studies (2017) shows that gravity affects the length of the cells' teleomeres. A telomere is the end section of a chromosome that protects the chromosome from deteriorating. Telomeres shorten as they replicate, and telomeres become shorter as we age. Shortened telomeres can negatively affect immune function, and reduced immunity can increase cancer susceptibility. In addition, if telomeres become too short our cells enter into a rapid aging state called senescence. Many age-related diseases are linked directly to shorted telomeres. Telomerase is an enzyme that can replenish the telomeres as explored in gravity testing studies, as well as through stem cell research that restores cells to an embryonic state. We also know that higher levels of Vitamin D and lower levels of CRP (C reactive protein) are linked to shortened telomere length, so reducing inflammation keeps our cells healthy and probably prolongs our lives. The best way to reduce inflammation is to cut out all processed foods, refined sugar and to increase exercise, but that will be covered in the next chapter.

Back to gravity healing, NASA's research shows that gravity can affect the cancer cells' dimension of growth as well as the cells' regeneration. If we can impose two-dimensional growth in cancer cells instead of three-dimensional growth, then we can control the cancer cells potentially without harmful effects to healthy cells. As we acquire ever-increasing knowledge, gravity healing will take us to a whole new scientific level of medicine.

And you might wonder what gravity has to do with the *Whole Foot Revolution*? Well, let me tell you. First, I believe that devices such as Tam's transducers might one day become more readily available to individuals wishing to use these modalities. Technology is improving every day and the positive healing results are what people are looking for to help improve their quality of life.

QUANTUM HEALING

You may have heard of quantum healing, especially from the best-selling book by Deepak Chopra called *Quantum Healing*. But, what does it mean? When we think of quantum we think of quantum mechanics as an area of theoretical physics. But how can you really heal from this quantum perspective? Quantum medicine is the future of medicine and there is currently a lot of science and research being performed on it and its role in healing.

Tied into theories on gravity healing is the concept of *quantum healing*—a phrase used by various physicians who practice integrative medicine. The field of integrative medicine is an approach to "whole person healing" that encompasses body, mind and spirit by encouraging healthy lifestyles. There are variations in each physician's concept of integrative medicine based on current research. Leaders in the field of quantum healing include Deepak Chopra, Andrew Weil, Mehmet Oz, and many other well-respected physicians.

Chopra's *Quantum Healing* (2015) shares stories of miraculous and even spontaneous healing when patients realize that we are not limited by our bodies (p. 9). Chopra points to cases in which even cancer has disappeared overnight—a healing state possibly triggered when patients shift their conscious attitude from a limited self-focused perspective to one that is more at one with the world. And while my book is not about "miracles" per se, miracles do occur all the time when we let go of limiting beliefs and embrace faith in the universe as a benevolent and healing source of wellness and abundance. There is plenty of evidence to support the healing power of our beliefs, from studies on placebo and nocebo effects (nocebo effects are when negative beliefs can actually kill you). There is a trend towards viewing ourselves as a "complete" or non-dual self that encompasses mind/body/spirit and connects us to the rest of the world. Quantum physics has proven through what is called the "observer effect" that thoughts affect matter, even when the matter is quite far from the thinker. Our thoughts do affect our healing.

Quantum physics has
proven through what is called
the "observer effect" that
thoughts affect matter, even
when the matter is quite far
from the thinker. Our thoughts
do affect our healing.

While in Boston for a Quantum Healing Seminar, I purchased a quantum wave healing machine. There were so many amazing stories about its results and the science made total sense to me. When I got back to Michigan, I thought I would try it on some of my patients to see if it helped with chronic pain and inflammation in the foot and ankle. Although I was intrigued by the claims, I was still skeptical of a machine that might reduce inflammation and pain.

BRITTANY HEALS HER HEEL

A 15-year old female named Brittany came into my office as a new patient with her mother and was complaining of severe pain to her right heel. She said it was very painful in the morning upon getting out of bed, and also painful when she sat for a while and stood back up. She said that it felt a little better as the day progressed, but the pain was nagging and was making it difficult for her to run and play soccer. Her pain was persistent for a few months and she hoped it would go away over time, but it didn't. She told me she was afraid of doctors and did not want any shots as she was afraid of needles. She also mentioned that she did not want any surgery.

Upon clinical and radiographic evaluation, she was diagnosed with a heel spur with plantar fasciitis to her right foot. I went through all the treatment options with her and since she was afraid of needles and didn't want any surgery I thought she would be the perfect candidate to test the quantum gravity wave machine. I asked Brittany and her mother if they were open to it and they were excited to try anything to make her feel better. I then had her sit for 15 minutes in the room with her right foot on top of the healing machine.

She said it felt better after the session, but she still had some discomfort and pain. I saw her for 2 more sessions and noticed improvements each time she came to the office. After her 3rd session I had her walk up and down the hallway and she could walk without any pain at all. I have to admit that I was pretty amazed with how quickly she became pain free. Out of curiosity I then took another x-ray of her foot and was absolutely shocked when I saw that the heel spur had gotten smaller and was almost completely gone. At this point, I was lost for words and felt that a miracle appeared before me.

I still remember the look on the patient and the mother when we looked at the x-rays and compared the two views. I did educate the mother and daughter on the cause of her condition and she had custom orthotics made to align her feet and prevent any reoccurrence of future foot problems. It was such an amazing feeling to be able to treat someone non-invasively and at that point I was a firm believer in quantum science and healing

THOUGHTS ARE THINGS

How our thoughts affect reality is a topic of growing interest in the Western world. Using our minds as an approach to non-traditional healing can be found in the work of Amit Goswami—the quantum physicist featured in *What the Bleep* and other films—as he writes in *Quantum Doctor* (2011) that the time is ripe for a new application of science that is rooted in consciousness. As a physicist and philosopher, Goswami explains that what we think can affect matter based somewhat on the "observer effect." The observer effect is the theory that the mere act of observing an object or situation changes the phenomenon.

Although these experiments go back to the 1800's in the Western world, experiments done with the Higgs boson particle in recent years caused the directors of the experiments to separate scientists while the collider was running. In those historic experiments, physicist at one end of the Haldron Collider (LHC) in France were separated from physicists at the other end, for concern that their conversations would affect the particles in motion. Goswami's many books reflect the idea that science does not create the universe, but that conscious creates everything that we perceive. It has taken Western society a very long time to know what our ancestors knew so well.

FOOT NOTES

Quantum Awareness

Notice your thoughts and their relationship to things. First you may have the thought—I am hungry and want a sandwich.

You then think where you can get the sandwich and then you find yourself eating the sandwich. It all started out with a thought.

Our thoughts are so powerful in this world. I even educate my patients on the importance of their thoughts in helping with their pain and condition. Having positive thoughts are so essential in producing positive results.

THE MYSTERIOUS QUANTUM REALITY

From a quantum physics perspective, quantum entanglement theory suggests that particles or objects are linked together such that the link bridges the space between them. Changes in one object's quantum state determines changes in the other object's quantum state regardless of how far away they are from each other. For example, a hypothetical pair of entangled coins will always land matching heads or tails even if they are flipped in different locations. Einstein referred to quantum entanglement as "spooky action at a distance." This theory might seem bizarre, but it is proving in a way why praying for another person might help them heal.

In 2003, researchers Rollin McCraty, Dana Atkinson, and Mike Tomasino at the HeartMath Institute showed that the physical structure of DNA can be altered by thought and intention. Our mind and our consciousness can change even our DNA. Dr. Masaru Emoto discovered that when concentrated thoughts are directed toward water, the shape of the water when photographed as ice crystals, change according to the thoughts. Negative thoughts create terrible looking crystals, while thoughts of love or compassion create well balanced and symmetrical structures. Since our bodies are the three quarters water, this research has been taken seriously by many scientists worldwide.

Adding to the argument, the work of Dr. Bruce Lipton at San Francisco State University refers to the experience of thoughts creating reality as the "biology of belief." Many doctors believe that genes cause or contribute to the generation of cancer cells because certain types of cancer seem to run in families. That is why doctors ask for your medical history and also the history of your parents, grandparents, and siblings. For instance, if a woman had breast cancer, her daughter is at increased risk for breast cancer. The transferring mechanism is hereditary genes. Imagine the possibilities if we can change DNA by virtue of our beliefs!

ALLAN'S LAST HOPE

Allan was a 62-year old diabetic who came to my office with chronic non-healing diabetic ulceration on the bottom of his left foot. He was treated by three other doctors prior to seeing me, without any success. He was discouraged and frightened because family members and close friends who were also diabetic suffered amputations due to the destruction of healthy tissue from the lack of blood flow to limbs. He told me that I was his last hope and he was starting to think that his foot would never heal. He started to believe that he would eventually need an amputation like his other diabetic friends. He also told me that the last doctor he saw told him that the amputation was probably inevitable, and yet he came to see me for one last opinion.

I could see from his face and his energy field that he was in total fear and on the verge of giving up. He also seemed depressed, which is a detriment to healing. I calmed him down and told him to think positive thoughts about his life and to spend a little time every day visualizing that his foot was healing. It seems to me that many books suggest "meditation" but many patients aren't sure how to go about that. They need to know what to meditate on, so in this case, seeing a healthy and happy foot seemed like the best possible visualization. Up to this point, Allan was visualizing an amputated foot, reinforcing his negative beliefs!

After I evaluated him and took x-rays of his foot, I was confident that the ulcer could heal. I noticed that one of the bones in his foot–called a metatarsal–was causing pressure when he walked. By decreasing the pressure of the bone on the ulcer, and with proper wound care, I believed that his foot would heal, especially since he had adequate circulation in the foot.

We did a simple procedure to elevate the bone in the foot to offload the ulcer and continued with wound care. I gave Allan hope that if he spent time with a healthier lifestyle to control his diabetes, and with a better attitude focused on health and happiness, he would get better. Every time Allan returned for follow up visits–especially when the ulcer was getting better–his attitude became more positive. You could actually see relief on his face and in his overall body. Can you imagine that it never occurred to him to visualize a healthy foot? He only had the scary and negative stories in his head until that point. Within 3 weeks the patient was totally healed of his ulcer, and our sessions together inspired him to eat healthier foods, walk more, and meditating a little. He was so excited to regain hope about his life. This is one good example of how our mind and attitude can play a major role in our bodies healing and by having a positive mindset and positive attitude can help us heal. When we allow our fear and emotions to get in the way of our health, it can have a negative consequence and impact on our healing.

Chapter Six

ALIGNMENT

Think of the magic of that foot, comparatively
small, upon which your whole weight rests.
It's a miracle, and the dance is a celebration of
that miracle.
- Martha Graham

IT'S A BALANCING ACT

*Think of the magic of that foot, comparatively small,
upon which your whole weight rests. It is a miracle.*
- Martha Washington

Have you ever experienced driving your car where your wheels
were out of alignment and how it affected the driving and steer-
ing of the car? Misaligned wheels will eventually cause wear and
tear damage to your car and also on its performance. This is very
similar to us walking with misaligned feet which will eventually
cause wear and tear damage to the rest of our body. As I stated

previously, it is so important for each of us to be aligned with our mind, body, and sole.

Misaligned wheels will eventually cause wear and tear damage to your car and also on its performance. This is very similar to us walking with misaligned feet which will eventually cause wear and tear damage to the rest of our body

One of the primary purposes of feet is balance. I care about how well our bodies balance on our feet. It is a fact that people rarely think about the alignment of their feet until they have pain, and that is a mistake that I am hoping to correct with the *Whole Foot Revolution.*

As a kid, I played soccer, but I wore my brother's cleats which were a little bigger than what I should have worn. Not realizing that his shoes had worn out to accommodate his own misalignment, I developed a knife-like pain in the bottom of my foot and up into my heel. Every time I woke up in the morning and got out of bed I suffered. It was a nagging pain at it affected my everyday activities. I was cranky, and I was miserable.

From wearing shoes aligned to someone else's body, I had extra strain on the bottom area of my feet where a thick ligament called the plantar fascia runs. Running in my brother's shoes put extra strain on the ligament which radiated pain from the bottom of my foot to my heel. I was treated by a foot specialist with an injection of cortisone in the area to calm down the pain, but looking back, we all know that cortisone doesn't solve the problem, it just covers it up for a while.

When I describe the importance of proper foot alignment to my patients, I often compare our feet to the tires on our car. If our tires are out of alignment, we can have many problems when we drive including damage to the tires or even an accident. This is not unlike having feet out of alignment.

SIGNS OF MISALIGNMENT

Some of the symptoms of misaligned feet include arthritis, bunions, heel pain, hammer toes, neuromas, nerve entrapments, neuropathy, tarsal tunnel syndrome, tendonitis, growing pains in children and teens, ankle instability and sprains, knee problems, hip pain, back pain, shoulder pain, neck pain, migraines, and even TMJ (for more information about specific foot problems, download my free e-book guide to healthy feet at www. WholeFootRevolution.com). If you suffer from any of the above, I would suggest that you find a great foot specialist who understands proper alignment so that you can adjust your posture and start living with more flexibility and better overall health.

Exercise is essential to our overall health and wellness because it helps increase our metabolism which burns calories and it also improves our mental well-being. Walking is one of the best forms of exercise because it is easy, inexpensive, and it doesn't require any special equipment other than a properly fitting pair of walking shoes. A sedentary person takes about 3,000 steps per day and a moderately active person takes approximately 7,000 steps. Active people can take more than 10,000. When you are out of alignment, every step you take is adding to the problem.

A sedentary person takes about 3,000 steps per day and a moderately active person takes approximately 7,000 steps.

FOOT NOTES

Alignment Check Up

Inspect your shoes to look for where you are out of alignment.

I suggest you take your shoes and put them flat on the ground. I would then look at the back of the shoe at the heel area and see if there are any wear patterns.

Similar to a tire on a car, when your car is out of alignment it will cause abnormal wear patterns in the tread of the tire. Our shoes are big indicators in telling us if our feet and body are out of balance and misaligned.

For instance, if you look at the back of your shoe and you notice wear pattern and breakdown on the outside of the heel, you know that you have pronation and misalignment of your ankle bone on your heel bone causing abnormal wear patterns in your shoes, similar to the analogy of wear patterns on your tires of your car. In other words, your shoes never lie!

If you suffer with pain as you walk or do exercise, your body is telling you that there is something wrong. People are told by their doctors to exercise and walk, but a lot of patients–especially those who are sedentary–stop moving because of pain. But good health depends on exercise, so we should really only stop long enough to find help so that we can keep moving! Spending extra time wiggling your toes, pointing them, circling them, massaging them, and doing yoga or exercises in bare feet will also help them become stronger and healthier. Even bed ridden individuals can move their feet while laying down!

When we stand, walk, or run, excessive force is placed on the joints, ligaments, and tendons of our feet, knees, hips, and back. Many active people who walk or stand all day also have more pain in all parts of their body, particularly if they suffer from inflammation due to diet. Many have surgery to repair various wear-and-tear damage only to discover a reoccurrence of the same symptoms. The leading complication of foot, knee, and back surgery is reoccurrence. Paying attention to the feet and addressing the misalignment is the best solution.

PRONATION AND HYPERPRONATION

Foot misalignment is not a condition you can outgrow; it will continue to get worse as you get older. Human beings need a little bit of movement in our feet to help our foot adapt to uneven surfaces and terrain. However, if you have excessive abnormal motion in the foot–a condition known as over pronation or hyper pronation–you will probably experience foot pain or instability of the ankle, problems with your knees, hips, and lower back. When we over pronate, the ankle bone dislocates from the heel bone and this hind foot dislocation causes a chain reaction up the body causing a flattening of the arch in certain patients, and stabbing pain in others.

SHIN SPLINTS

Shin splints are a reaction by the muscles of the leg bone from misalignment of the feet. The misalignment causes an extra pull and over working on the muscles and tendons of the leg bone. The strain causes inflammation which can be very painful.

For children, the pain is usually pronounced in the evening because they have stopped running around and notice that their legs hurt. Pediatricians sometimes call this a "growing pain," but it is a shin splint condition caused by foot misalignment.

Pain is a warning sign that something is wrong. Runners can also acquire shin splints. Runners with misaligned feet are working ten times harder than necessary, and their body is literarily crying for help.

STEVE RUNS A MARATHON

Steve, an active young man came to my office complaining of severe pain to both his legs from shin splints. He is a very avid runner and has been training for the *Free Press Marathon* here in Detroit. The marathon was 2 weeks away and he was concerned that he wouldn't be able to run in the marathon as he couldn't bear the pain. I educated the patient about a great non-invasive thirty-minute treatment utilizing grounding patches to help expedite his healing in order to help him become pain free and be able to participate and run in the marathon. Steve told me he was open to do anything in order to help alleviate his pain and allow him to run. After his 2nd treatment of placing grounding pads on his painful shins attached to grounding electrical outlet in the wall, he was feeling a lot better but still having a little pain to his shins. We then did another grounding treatment on him and he was 100% pain free and able to run without any pain. He was so excited that he was pain-free and able to run in the marathon.

BUNIONS

If you take off your shoes and socks and notice you have a bump on the inside of your big toe joint that sometimes causes some discomfort when you wear shoes, you may have what is called a bunion.

Bunions are bumps on the inside of the big toe joint. They are caused from misaligned feet, and with time, the deformity of the bunion will worsen. In the next phase, the ankle bone displaces from the heel causing more pressure and strain to the big toe joint. Orthopedics education teaches us that the hind foot controls the forefoot. Misalignment of the ankle bone and the heel has to be corrected to solve the problem. The biggest problem with bunions (besides discomfort) is reoccurrence so adjusting the hind foot is the solution. Once we address the underlying cause a lot of the mild bunions will reposition themselves or be easily removed.

HEEL PAIN

One of the most common complaints I hear in my practice is heel pain. Heel pain starts with the overall misalignment and mechanics of the foot. When the plantar fascia fibers are strained, it will cause mild tears that cause pain with every step.

Over two million dollars per year are spent for the treatment of heel pain. Most often, the symptoms are addressed by injecting cortisone into the inflammation and/or cleaning out the inflammation using a surgical procedure. However, if the pathology of misaligned feet continues, the plantar fascia will continue to stretch and will eventually rupture again.

Over two million dollars per year is spent for the treatment of heel pain.

FOOT NOTES

Healing Your Heels

Healing your heels can be helped with a few simple exercises. First get yourself a tennis ball, cold plastic water bottle, or a foot roller. Then place it into the freezer for about 5 minutes so it's nice and cold.

Now sit in a comfortable chair and put whatever object you decided to use on the ground. Take your shoes and socks off.

Now place your foot on top of the cold rolling object and roll it up and down the bottom of your foot and heel area for about 10-15 minutes. You can watch television while you do this exercise as it will make the time go by fast. This rolling back and forth technique will allow the fibers on the bottom of the foot to stretch out. In addition, the cold temperature will help to alleviate inflammation and also help to stretch the tight plantar fascia bands on the bottom of the foot.

After the stretching exercise, I would recommend you apply arnica gel to the entire bottom of your feet. You can also rub in some peppermint essential oil which will help with the pain. I would suggest you perform this heel stretching exercise at least twice daily. I would suggest you do the heel stretching exercises in the morning and in the evening. I would continue doing these exercises daily.

How does your heel feel after this exercise?

SCIATICA AND NEUROPATHY AS A MANIFESTATION OF MISALIGNED FEET

Patients with sciatica complain of shooting pains from their buttock into their thigh and down their leg to their feet. The patient usually experiences a tingly and burning sensation with some neurologic pain that lingers and persists. Men sometimes acquire sciatica from placing their wallets in their back pockets. As they sit down, the wallet compresses on the sciatic nerve and the nerve gets compressed and inflamed. In addition, some patients have misalignment in their feet which causes disruption of their lumbar-4 and lumbar-5 regions in their lower back due to impingement and entrapment as well as inflammation of the nerve. Misaligned feet can also cause nerve inflammation in the feet—a condition called neuroma and tarsal tunnel syndrome neuropathy, which cause burning, numbness, and shooting pains in the feet and legs.

Like the roots of a tree, the feet are the foundation to our entire musculoskeletal system. As the Chinese say, a tree dies from its roots, so it is important to take care of our feet.

I have seen many patients who visit a chiropractor two or three times per week and still have problems with pain. Upon evaluation of their feet, I noted that they had a misalignment of both feet that was having impact not only with the pain of the feet but also with other parts of the body.

ORTHOTICS

Many people do not think about orthotics unless they are running long distance or downhill skiing on a regular basis. In my own case, due to the foot issues I developed as a kid playing soccer, I was cast for custom orthotics devices that were placed inside my shoes. The orthotics put my feet into proper alignment and decreased the strain on the plantar fascia. My pain diminished after utilizing my custom orthotics daily and lessened more after I purchased new soccer cleats that were the correct size. Because of my own suffering, I understand what it feels like when a patient comes in with heel pain associated with plantar fasciitis due to improperly aligned feet.

As we walk, there is displacement and dislocation of the ankle bone (talus) on our heel bone (calcaneus). This displacement causes instability in the midfoot and forefoot areas. When the displacement, or talotarsal dislocation, occurs, the tendons, ligaments, bones, and muscles all displace and cause strain. Because these bones, tendons and ligaments are forced to operate from positions that are unnatural, foot and ankle problems usually arise, as well as problems within the rest of the body such as neck and back pain. Since our feet are the most distal part of our body and are mobile adapters which we utilize every day for getting around, stability of the feet and proper alignment are the key to overall health and might even be the key to happiness! Orthotics can help in some circumstances.

FEETALIGN™ PROCEDURE

There is a unique solution to resolve the displacement of the ankle on the heel. By inserting a titanium stent between the ankle bone and the heel bone in a naturally occurring space called the sinus tarsi, the normal range of motion and stabilization of the ankle without excessive movement is restored. The FeetAlign™ procedure is performed on patients from age three up into their 90's, is a minimally invasive, and takes approximately fifteen minutes to perform. The patient comes in with misaligned feet and walks out with a permanently aligned foot. There is no more need for reconstructive surgery that involves cutting bones, fusions, screws, and plates. The FeetAlign™ procedure is similar to correcting a closed artery in a heart patient when a stent is placed into the artery to open it up. With the misaligned foot, the sinus tarsi is closed or collapsed. By placing the stent between the ankle and heel bones and holding that space open, it prohibits excessive movement, stabilizes of the rear foot, and forms an arch for patients who have flat feet.

While custom orthotics will help to control the heel and put that in a neutral position, orthotics can't correct the pathology of misaligned feet. FeetAlign realigns the foot structure internally so that the ankle bone does not displace while walking. It's like creating a permanent, built in orthotic, that enables people to walk barefoot without discomfort, and creates an arch where there wasn't one. This simple procedure allows them to have a normal biomechanical foot structure and foundation that will also correct ankle instability and issues with the knees, hip, and lower back, it will help to realign and put all those joints into their normal anatomical position.

RAJ IN THE SKY

Raj, a young man from Toronto, Canada came to my office reporting that I was his last hope. An airline pilot for Air Canada he said that he might have to give up his passion for flying because of the chronic pain that he was having in his feet, knees, and back. He told me that his research on the internet led him to testimonials of patients on *YouTube* that had similar symptoms to himself and were now living a pain-free, active lifestyle. He had been treated by other doctors in Canada for many years without relief. He was told that nothing further could be done to help, and his option was chronic pain or medication to cover the pain. He flew all the way from Toronto, Canada to my office in Michigan to be evaluated one last time. He was very depressed and emotional during his consultation. He stated that he could barely longer walk through the terminals because of the severe pain.

His fear was that he would have to retire from flying. I was very shocked when I questioned him if any of the doctors performed a gait analysis on him. He didn't know what I meant by gait analysis and when I explained it to him he seemed optimistic. I then educated him on a very underdiagnosed condition which I have been seeing in patients which was causing his chronic pain to his feet and musculoskeletal system. As I performed my clinical evaluation and gait analysis found that he had very misaligned feet. I then had him look in a mirror so that he could see the back of his feet and how his heel rotated outward and how his arch was collapsed down to the ground. This was very eye-opening for him especially after I showed him what a normal foot should look like. I then performed dynamic fluoroscopy imaging in the office where he could see the bones in his feet and ankle in action live on the computer screen.

As he placed weight on his feet he saw the displacement and shift of his ankle bone (talus) on his heel bone (calcaneus). I explained to him that the foot is the foundation to the entire musculoskeletal system and when the foot is out of alignment it will cause misalignment to the knee, hips, back, shoulders and entire musculoskeletal system. He was so ecstatic and excited that someone actually found the root cause of his problem. I also educated him on different treatment modalities to help with his misalignment of his feet. Since he had an internal structural bone misalignment, custom orthotics were not enough to address the displacement of the ankle on the heel bone since the major pathology is proximal to where the custom orthotics control in the foot. He stated that he had three different custom orthotics made for him and none of them ever helped his chronic pain problem.

I then explained to him a particular procedure which prevents the displacement of the ankle bone on the heel bone and provides a permanent realigned foot and solution to his problem. After a week of performing the FeetAlign procedure on him, he reported a big difference and improvement in the foot that was performed in comparison to the other foot. I then performed the FeetAlign procedure on his other foot and he was able to get around postoperatively without any major pain or discomfort. I then had him do icing and elevation as well as some physical therapy exercises for the next month. When he came for his final visit, he was like a whole new man. He was happy, pain free, and looked very good. He was so appreciative about changing his life and most importantly for allowing him to continue his passion and love of being a pilot for Air Canada. He gave me a big hug and said, "Thank you Dr. Weinert for giving me my life back." I started to tear up as it really hit home to me on the impact we can all have on one other. That is why I love what I do. Whenever I can change someone's life through the gift I was given I know that they in turn can use their gifts to spread healing to others too.

SUPPORT INSERTS

Support inserts come prepackaged and placed inside your shoe. You can go to almost any pharmacy or chain store and purchase non-prescription arch supports. They are frequently advertised on TV by marketing pitchmen in white coats; who clearly are not doctors.

When you think you are ordering custom orthotics online, you are buying the same nonprescription shoe inserts, but at a hefty price not covered by your insurance. Despite what the ads may lead you to believe, as a doctor who has spent his career dedicated solely to feet, I ask you to use simple common sense when self-diagnosing your foot needs and consider what I and many other reputable doctors have learned from years of experience treating hundreds of patients with great success.

You can have success with over-the-counter products made by Dr. Scholl's and other such companies, and you may never have to see a foot doctor your entire life. However, an advertisement, no matter how convincing, cannot treat a foot issue the way a doctor can. In the same way that children and adults get braces to straighten their teeth, I suggest that you get evaluated to see if inserts will work or consider what type of custom orthotics can straighten out your feet.

SHOES GLORIOUS SHOES

When I was growing up my mother would take us to a shoe store when we needed new shoes. There, the person would measure our feet, ask questions and make recommendations based on what the measurements said before selling us a pair of shoes. Nowadays, we go to places like Target, Walmart and sporting goods stores and buy things directly off the rack. Especially now with computers and technology, many people are going online to places like Zappos to buy their shoes. By doing this, how do we know we are getting the right footwear and most importantly the proper size? The answer is, we don't.

Back in the old days, shoes were made exclusively to fit the size of the individual foot. As a matter of fact, the idea of covering one's foot dates back 40,000 years ago to the Middle Paleolithic. Most shoes were more like wrap around sandals without and heels or arches. By the 1800s shoes began to be differentiated between male and female by color, style and fabric, but it wasn't until 1850s that shoes were made with no differentiation from left and right shoes.

As the twentieth progressed, so did the variations of the shoes. Women's shoes became more arched and delicate heels grew higher and narrower.

A survey conducted by the American Podiatric Medical Association showed that about 40 percent of women admitted to wearing shoes they liked, even if they caused them discomfort.

To this day, women's heels continue to create serious foot problems as many women will choose fashion over comfort. A survey conducted by the American Podiatric Medical Association showed that about 40 percent of women admitted to wearing shoes they liked, even if they caused them discomfort. Seventy-three percent admitted to already having shoe-related foot issues, thinking they were just normal occurrences. But experiencing foot pain is NOT normal. More than 43 million Americans have foot problems. Many feel the pain is serious enough to seek medical attention. Some people just think the pain will go away. Many will look back and regret not having had something done, especially when foot deformities set in later in life. They regret buying and wearing shoes only because they were fashionable or on the clearance rack.

As long as shoe designers continue to design fashionable high heels, women will continue to buy them. For many women, high heels are shoes that are worn for specific occasions, for others they could spend an eight-hour day on heels. So, if I am speaking to you, here a few tips that could save your feet.

FOOT NOTES

Shoe Inspection

I would recommend you go through your closet and look at all the shoes in your shoe collection.

If there are any shoes that have wear patterns in the heels and diminished support in the arches, I would look into investing in a new pair to save your feet and body from suffering with chronic pain. Just like we have to change our worn-out tires on our car from wear and tear, we have to do the same with our shoes to prevent wear and tear on our feet and body.

TIPS FOR HIGH HEELS

Get the best fitting high heels possible. Shoes should conform to the shape of your foot. Your foot should never, ever conform to the shape of the shoes. Don't get them just because they are on sale! If a shoe doesn't fit when you try it on, it isn't going to fit when you get home. I always recommend shopping for shoes in the afternoon because your feet gradually swell the longer you are on them.

If you do a lot of city walking you need shoes with good shock absorption. Just like your car you need to handle the bumps. Cushion, cushion and cushion again! Shoe inserts can help, but you can get pain in the ball of the foot from standing in your heels for a long time. There is a lot of pressure on the ball, so I recommend investing in really inexpensive over the counter silicone gel metatarsal pads.

Try to wear an open toe high heel that helps to alleviate the pressure on the toes, especially if you already have corns or calluses. This will help prevent them from getting worse and may be more comfortable for you. Wearing high heels can have an impact not only on your foot and ankle but on the rest of your body. This pressure can lead to nerve issues like Morton's neuroma, which can cause numbness or a tingling sensation in between the toes or on the ball of the foot.

This can also lead to Haglund's deformity, which is a bony enlargement on the back of the heel often referred to as "pump bump." This often leads to bursitis (inflammation of the bursa, which is a fluid filled sack between the tendon and bone). Wearing high heels can also lead to hammertoes, which you may remember as abnormal bending of the joints. Statistics show that over 60 percent of women who regularly wear heels have reported having some type of heel or ankle pain.

We also see knee pain as the heels get higher. The more stress that is generated on the inside of the knee the more the resulting compression will eventually damage your cartilage and promote arthritis or degenerative joint disease. Additional statistics show that, on average, it takes females only about thirty minutes before they start having some sort of discomfort. This is why you'll often see women taking their shoes off during wedding receptions or during other long events.

Wearing high-heeled boots can cause a lot of strain to the Achilles tendon and eventually lead to tendonitis. If you experience pain, try some over-the-counter cushions or wearing boots with a thicker heel. Also, try to change the height of your shoe each day by alternating your shoes. This will help your feet and extend the life of your favorite pumps, so you can buy more! Better to purchase heels that have a gradual slope instead of some of the four-inch heels that give you a straight drop down to the flatbed portion of the shoe. The gradual slope will offer more stability and will be a lot easier on the arch while decreasing some of the pain in the ball of the foot.

Wearing a thicker heel will be a lot easier on the arch and will also help alleviate any pain you may experience. Doing this will provide better balance, relieve pressure and offer improved weight distribution. A thicker heel will help to relieve pressure by distributing the weight on your foot more evenly and will allow for better balance; in addition, it will help to reduce problems with your Achilles tendon, such as tendonitis. High heels have the tendency to slip in the front. Many times, you see a gap when a woman is walking that is big enough to fit a cell phone in. This is not a normal fitting shoe. Heels that don't fit properly also cause the front of the foot to slide forward, creating more pressure, discomfort and pain to the toes.

The simple truth is that if you are an athlete at any level you are more prone to having foot problems. It is open season on the foot when engaging in sporting activities, opening up the door to bone, skin, ligament, muscle and cartilage issues in the foot. People at all ages participate in a wide variety of sporting activities. You should always be careful when engaging in any sport as there are no surefire ways to avoid potential injuries. This is why it is essential to have the proper footwear for the specific sport. I would recommend children participating in sports to have their feet measured and sized every 6 months as their feet go through growth spurts and their shoe sizes change.

I have seen several professional athletes that have severe damage to their feet from playing their respective sport. For instance, football players have a common problem in the big toe joint which is called "turf toe." This happens a lot with football players. It occurs when there is an increase in what we call "dorsiflexion," which occurs when we flex our foot and the big toe goes upwards. It is very important for any athlete to be measured and fitted for shoes by a professional. In addition, athletes need to make sure their respective shoe corresponds with their sport and also their foot structure and biomechanics.

CHAPTER 7

WHOLE BODY NUTRITION AND HEALTH

I still have my feet on the ground,
I just wear better shoes.
-Oprah Winfrey

DIET & EXERCISE

There are currently over 10,000 books listed on Amazon on the topic of diet and health. There are millions on the topic of health in general. It is a huge subject and the best of the books are based on the newest scientific studies proving that the cause of most of our illness today is from diet and stress. This chapter intends to inform those who are engaged in the *Whole Foot Revolution* to look seriously at the implications of what goes into their bodies as a critical first step in regaining their health. Since this is only one chapter on a topic that many are writing entire books on, you won't find all the solutions here.

We strongly suggest that you consider this chapter as a springboard to find ways of eating that are sustainable for good health. That being said, if you have headaches, TMJ, arthritis, cancer, diabetes, heart disease, allergies, mood and or memory issues (or problems with your feet!), then you absolutely must look at the foods that you are eating, as well as how you handle stress. For instance, after a rough day in the world do you come home and have a big glass of wine? Or do you put your feet up and mindlessly drink a few beers and eat a full bag of chips? Do you still occasionally eat fast food lunches? Do you eat while on the run, never really noticing what it is that you are putting into your mouth?

I highly encourage everyone to focus on this issue. There is so much research out there today about the effect of food on the brain and body that it doesn't make sense that many ignore scientific facts in order to keep supporting bad habits. But if your health isn't stellar and your moods aren't idea, it would be beneficial to check out some of the newest diet and nutrition books that include both scientific evidence, AND delicious recipes to make your transition into health a wonderful experience.

Common logic, nutritionists and doctors focused on alternative health like Dr. Andrew Weil have seen the demise of our health due to diet and have been pointing to a return to a plant-based, organic diet for some time, but the trend is really gaining visibility with mainstream audiences now. While many developing countries eat what is now commonly called "the Mediterranean diet" (meals comprised mostly of vegetables with some fish or meat and lots of olive oil), in the 50s the US developed a trend of mass produced, artificially manufactured "foods" such as boxed cereals, canned foods, fast foods, processed snacks like chips, bagged candy and cookies, sugary soft drinks, and highly processed meats.

All of these foods fill our bodies with poisonous sugars, artificial ingredients, empty calories and toxic ingredients. The Mediterranean diet on the other hand, which has been shown to reduce inflammatory markers such as CRP and IL-6, reduce inflammation in the body. Some of the longest living and most beautiful people in the world live off very simple and healthy diets.

The result of artificially flavored, sugar coated food is a generation of adults with soaring rates of heart disease, cancer, diabetes, obesity, and dementia.

America is also notorious for launching the trend of "super-sized," empty calorie meals including double patty hamburgers on artificially manufactured white buns, French fries soaked in sugar to make them extra crispy (and fried in rancid, poor quality oil), giant milkshakes (made with fake milk and artificial ingredients), and soft drinks (a completely chemical concoction). The result of this dietary catastrophe is a generation of adults with soaring rates of heart disease, cancer, diabetes, obesity, and dementia.

The United States currently ranks #2 in the world for Alzheimer's, a debilitating disease that atrophies the brain and erases memory. There are an estimated 15.9 million over the age of 65 suffering from full blown Alzheimer's (cited from "*Forecasting the Global Burden of Alzheimer's*," Brookmeyer, Johnson, et al) and an estimated 200,000 who will develop early onset (before the age of 65). It is estimated that by 2050, the incidence will triple, costing taxpayers billions of dollars and causing endless suffering for patients and families.

There is plenty of evidence-based science being published every year that proves that the vast majority of these diseases can be prevented or possibly reversed through diet and exercise if intervention happens early enough and the number one way to either delay or negate the problem is through diet and exercise. Most underdeveloped countries such as India have *no incidence of Alzheimer's*, a fact attributed to a diet rich in vegetables and anti-inflammatory foods, despite the high rates of pollution, overpopulation, and stress due to a changing environment.

The underlying cause of most diseases is inflammation, which is the hottest topic in the wellness debate today. Inflammation is the body's response to foreign invaders. During an inflammatory response, our bodies increase its production of white blood cells, immune cells, and cytokines that help fight infection. When inflammation is caused by a mosquito bite for instance, classic signs include redness, pain, heat, and swelling.

Long term or chronic inflammation often occurs inside the body without noticeable symptoms until damage is done. When we douse our bodies day and night with high levels of sugar (that includes all simple carbohydrates such as white potatoes, white flour and alcohol that do not have fiber and convert quickly into sugar) our bodies break down. The process might start with packing on a few extra pounds or developing migraines. It might initially show up as joint pain or mood swings. This type of inflammation leads eventually to diseases such as cancer, diabetes, heart disease, fatty liver, and depression.

Current research shows that in our preindustrial past, humans were consuming over 150 grams of fiber per day obtained from whole, unprocessed foods, and virtually no sugar. Today, humans eat less that 15 grams of fiber (at least in industrialized societies) and are eating mostly foods that convert quickly into sugar in the body. This wreaks havoc on the immune system and destroys the body's ability to work at its optimum level. Not only do you gain weight and disease, but you end up feeling bad all the time, suffering from fatigue or headaches when you are living in a cycle of inflammation. Inflammation also makes you prone to serious infectious diseases.

The number one cause of inflammation is diet, and those suffering from severe inflammation (as revealed from various blood tests that check for inflammation rates) can begin to see relief within weeks of adjusting their diet. Once high inflammatory foods are replaced with immune boosting foods and supplements—and a healthier lifestyle including all the other revolutionary ideas found in this book—you can re-boot your system and get back on the road to health. It is our responsibility as humans given our truly amazing minds and bodies to take care of them, and for many of us it is as simple as getting educated and making the right choices to enhance wellness and restore the joy that is intrinsic to human life. You will shed unwanted pounds, get rid of acne and allergies, prevent devastating diseases, get off unnecessary and expensive meds that are covering up symptoms, and best of all, you will have happy, healthy feet that will take you everywhere! But one thing is for sure. You can't fix your problems with your feet or with your mind or with your heart by one approach alone. We are complex organisms that require a holistic approach to wellness, and that is why we wrote the *Whole Foot Revolution*.

INFLAMMATORY FOODS

For those of you who don't know about the inflammation/diet link, this chapter might help you start to eliminate a few things that will make a difference. A short list of foods that trigger inflammation include the following:

Refined sugar including: sugar, agave, molasses, cane juice, fructose, malt, dextrose, brown rice syrup, fruit juice, date sugar, glucose solids, barley malt, corn syrup, sucrose, coconut sugar and honey. Refined sugar is found in every type of pre-packaged food, from sweets to cereal to salad dressing. Avoid it like the plague!

Trans fats (partially hydrogenated oils) including margarine, corn oil, soybean oil, safflower oil. All bags of chips, breads, cookies, cakes, and more contain this ingredient which is directly linked to inflammatory disease such as heart disease and cancer.

Processed carbohydrates (refined flours and grains, particularly corn and wheat). These culprits are causing huge allergic responses in people and should be cut out entirely from a healthy diet.

High histamine foods corn, red wine, beer, gluten, and non-organic foods grown with pesticides, smoked meats, many fermented foods.

Excessive alcohol daily consumption and/or mixed drinks, wine, beer.

Processed meats including sausage, bacon, ham, canned meats, and prepackaged "lunch" meats.

FOOTNOTES

Pantry Inventory

I would suggest that you open up your refrigerator and read all the labels. I bet you will be surprised at what is in a lot of the items that you never had a clue on. How many times do you actually read the labels of foods and beverages you are getting while shopping in the store?

I would also suggest that you take out the foods in your cupboards and read them and educate yourself on the ingredients and if they are organic or not and if they contain the inflammatory items that were discussed. We need to be familiar with what we are putting in our bodies and need to be proactive with our diets and nutrition.

We need to rid inflammatory foods from our diet. After all, "You are what you eat!" If you eat crappy you will feel crappy. And if you eat good you will feel good.

GLUTEN SENSITIVITY

About more than 20 years, there has been a trend towards high complex carbohydrate diets that influenced a daily diet of cereal, whole grain bread or bagels, rice, and other seemingly "healthy" grains. Today, a record number of people are developing allergies to grains, and allergies are of course, inflammation. Many immune specialists are now advocating a diet packed with vegetables and healthy fish, some meat, and healthy oils, and limited amounts of whole grains with little or zero flour-based products due to gluten sensitivities and the destruction that gluten can cause on bodies. Research and books on paleo diets and "Whole30" are changing the way many eat by providing delicious recipes that are easy to prepare, cost effective, and truly healing.

FOOD SENSITIVITY TESTING

When it comes to health, each person is completely customized and unique. However, some things are universally beneficial when it comes to good health. It is always best to check with your doctor or research it for yourself so that you are comfortable with it. After so many years of studying health and being my own health advocate, these are some things I cannot live without. They have been life changing. Of course, it goes without saying that each person is individual and there is no one-size fits all. It is always best to see what resonates with you and research it, be your own healthcare advocate. See if it is something you should incorporate into your life and do what you feel is best for you. Here are a few that most can really benefit from.

One of the most important things that can be done is to get a food sensitivity test done. It turned out, my wife had 1 of the genes for Celiac disease. Apparently one gene is enough to cause major damage in the gut. Celiac disease is a serious autoimmune disease that can occur in genetically predisposed people where the ingestion of gluten leads to damage in the small intestine. Gluten is a general name for the protein found in wheat and many other grains. Gluten helps food retain their shape. It acts like the "glue" that holds food together. 2.5 million people are said to be undiagnosed with Celiac disease, according to Celiac disease foundation. They are said to be at risk for lifelong complications. Although my wife doesn't have Celiac disease, gluten still causes a major inflammatory response in the gut and over time will damage the gut as well. And there are many other people like my wife. If she never had that testing done, she would never have known, because the symptoms are silent.

You are not only what you eat, but what you absorb.

The attacks from gluten will damage the villi in the small intestine and eventually lead to a person not being able to absorb the nutrients that you eat. You are not only what you eat, but what you absorb. Check *Celiac.org* for a list of foods, also a list of foods you would not expect gluten to be in. Everywell is an at home sensitivity test you can find on *Everywell.com*. You can do the test in the privacy of your own home. Nutritional stress is something many people do not factor into their health. According the *American Psychological Association,* chronic stress is linked to 6 leading causes of death. Heart disease, cancer, lung ailments, accidents, suicide, etc. 75% of all doctor's office visits are stress related ailments and complaints. Nutritional stress is still a stress. Food can be very healing but for some of us, the wrong ones can be very damaging as well. Even foods that are deemed healthy. There are other testing companies you can use, this is just one example. I gave this information to several people. They decided to get the testing done. One person told me her face had broken out with acne horribly for many years. She did the food sensitivity testing and was amazed how much better she felt and how much more energy she had. One of the firsts things she noticed was that she immediately stopped breaking out.

These are just some of the benefits that can be achieved by knowing the right foods for you. I have countless stories like this one. Foods that you have an intolerance to, can cause headaches, skin problems, digestive issues, joint pain and more. Also, the things you cannot see like inflammation and immune responses. Making your immune system working much harder than it should. Don't focus on what you can't have, just focus on what you can and how much better you will look and feel.

SOLE WATER: TRACE MINERAL NUTRIENTS

Making healthy lifestyle choices are not always easy. I always say, just do a little bit at a time and eventually it will become a habit. Little habits can turn into big changes you can really see and feel. You will slip up, you will fall off the "health" wagon. But that's okay, just get right back up and start again. This health tip is easy and cheap! A highly beneficial habit to check into is something called "Sole." Sole is a salt water solution, made with filtered water and unrefined salt. It is essentially just water that has been fully saturated with natural, unrefined salt. Don't go and grab the Morton's in the big blue rounded box! That is not it! That is the fake, bleached toxic stuff that is not what you want. This has to be unrefined salt. Unrefined salt has so many trace minerals that we need and don't get. Various sources say 75 trace minerals, while others say more.

We have to undo what we have learned and that is, salt is so bad for us. Yes, the white/bleached junk is bad for us because they have removed all the nutrients, but not this. This has been around for centuries in many cultures. Some people like the Himalayan Salt, and others like the grey salt. There are different brands, and some are fine grains, some look like little rocks. There are many different brands as well, like Real Salt, Celtic, Himalayan. I have been doing sole water now for many years. I prefer the fine grain and also the grey salt. It has more of a "sweeter" taste and that makes it very easy to drink. The 'fine grain', makes it easier to dissolve quickly. They all work well, that just happens to be my personal preference.

Sole water helps the body to re-hydrate. It helps the body to detoxify as salt water/sole naturally removes bad bacteria. Sole boosts energy. The minerals in sole help to give so much nourishment to the body and that nourishment gives us energy. Unrefined salt/ sole is very healing for the adrenals too. Your adrenals need a lot of good salt and minerals to function properly. Add in stress, poor nutrition and too much sugar and they will struggle even more. Many people even battle severe adrenal fatigue, which can really make you feel really exhausted.

Chronic stress can make the adrenals release more cortisol and "burn out." A little stress is normal, but too much can cause a lot of strain on the adrenals. This helps to replace some of the minerals that the adrenals really need. Adrenals cannot produce the needed minerals and hormones without support. That is why sole is so great to help nourish the adrenals and recharging them with sole. Vitamin C is also very healing for the adrenals. You can squeeze in some fresh lemons to your sole mixture if you have adrenal fatigue issues. Acerola cherries have some of the highest amounts of Vitamin C. They make powders you can add as well. Always choose organic whenever humanly possible. It is not just the calories you have to count, but the chemicals too! To make the sole water solution, you just need a glass quart jar with a non-metal lid. I use the Aquasana glass bottles since it seems to be harder to find jars without metal lids. Uline.com has some as well. You add one cup of unrefined salt of your choice and fill up the jar with filtered water. Let it sit out overnight/24 hours. That's it! It is that simple and easy. You can store the sole' right on the counter as the salt be its own natural preservative.

Every morning on an empty stomach, take a teaspoon of the sole put that in a glass and then you add the rest with filtered water. I personally do this about 3 times daily, in between meals. You may have to work your way up. If it seems too salty, you can always add more filtered water. There are so many benefits to list, but one that I personally experienced outside of helping to heal my severe adrenal fatigue and energy is pain. My wife has severe endometriosis and unbearable pain that is associated with it. For whatever reason since doing the sole on a very regular basis, the normal excruciating pain that she gets from the disease is far less severe.

I am not sure why this is helping, but so grateful it is. For more information, I like the article from *Thefamilythathealstogether.com* and *Wellnessmama.com*. My personal hero, Dr. Brownstein's book *"Salt your way to health"* is another resource.

IODINE PROTOCOL

Almost 7 years ago, I stumbled across a protocol that I had never heard about before. I was just on social media and it was the first thing that popped up on my feed that day. I read the article, then the comments and was very intrigued. I was very interested in researching and learning more since my wife, Julie, has been suffering with thyroid problems and other health issues for many years. It was called the Iodine protocol. I grabbed every book I could get my hands on, including Dr. Brownstein's book (*"Iodine and Why You Need It, Why You Can't Live Without It"*) and Lynne Farrows book, *("The Iodine Crisis")*. I joined groups on Facebook, read through hours and hours of comments. So many people appeared to be having major healing responses to this protocol. I was so excited to find out about the iodine protocol and told my wife about it. She was so excited and started to do her own research on this amazing protocol before she started to implement it into her life.

Iodine is not only responsible for production of thyroid hormones, but the production of all hormones in the body. Adequate iodine levels are extremely important for proper immune function. Iodine contains potent antibacterial, anti-parasitic, antiviral and anti-cancer properties. Iodine used to be in a lot of our foods many years ago, but it was taken out and replaced with cheaper ingredients. Iodine is an essential element that is needed for life.

Iodine is a trace element that is naturally present in some foods, added to others and a dietary supplement.

According to *Livescience.com,* "Overall, Iodine deficiency affects 2 billion people worldwide." Some sources say more than that. Iodine supplementation can be individualized based on your various health conditions. Many people take just drops of the liquid form per day, while others take upwards to 50 milligrams to 100 milligrams or more, based on how they feel or if they have a more severe condition they are trying to treat. There always seems to be a debate about it. Some will say that too little iodine supplementation can cause more detox reactions, while others say higher doses provide less detox reactions. Julie went the "low and slow" route and had severe detox reactions with only 12.5 milligrams. For her, it was true that the lower doses did cause her more of a detox reaction. Each person should do exactly what they feel comfortable doing. Again, no one size fits all.

According to *Stop the Thyroid Madness* website, the guidelines for the other vitamins in the protocol are Selenium: 200 micrograms to 400 micrograms. A very important issue to note is that some people have a genetic defect called MTHFR. Many people like myself never knew I had this genetic issue. So, it is a very good idea for anyone supplementing with Selenium to have their levels checked before supplementing and checking them at least each year. Individuals with that genetic predisposition can build up toxic levels of selenium causing hair loss. I know people that only took 200 micrograms and still had an issue, even after they stopped. So, it is very important side effect to note. Magnesium: 400 milligrams to 1200 milligrams. Vitamin C: 3000 milligrams to 10,000 milligrams. Vitamins B2 and

B3 (ATP Co-factors) 100 milligrams of riboflavin and 500 milligrams of no flush niacin. Inositol hexinicotinate form 1-2 times per day. Unrefined Celtic salt at least 1 teaspoon per day.

Julie was told by her primary care doctor that she should not take Iodine because she has Hashimoto's autoimmune disease. But from *Stop the Thyroid Madness* site reports and from her personal experience, many people were doing very well on the Iodine protocol. Some will do the low and slow method, while others will start right off with 100 milligrams. It will just depend on how you feel and what you will find is best for you through your own research and being your own healthcare advocate. Julie was at 12.5 milligrams for 8 months and yes, she had detox symptoms including sweating profusely and itching like mad. Julie felt like she had more energy and that someone plugged her brain back in.

After 8 months, she went to 25 milligrams, stayed on that for a pretty short time and felt so great, and then wanted to see how she felt at 50 milligrams. She felt fine at that amount. She then started to experience heart palpitations. She then decided at that point to speak to an iodine literate practitioner. They can be very hard to find, but there was a listing online that she found, and she able to find one in our area. The practitioner told her that her adrenals must be suffering as her body is so deficient that her thyroid is "gobbling" up all the iodine and not leaving any for her adrenals. She was spot on, because going to 100 milligrams, her heart palpitations were completely gone. She has been going to the doctor for over 20 years. She not only felt just tired, but very exhausted every day. She kept going to the doctor who was running all these tests.

On paper, she was the picture of health, but she felt like walking death. She knew something was wrong and was on a mission to find help. Once she started taking the iodine protocol and the detox symptoms stopped, she had so much energy and felt amazing. This is why I share this story about my wife in hopes of helping others who may have a loved one, family member or colleague suffering through a similar health situation. Seeing Julie struggle for 20 years of feeling awful and nobody able to figure out was causing her problems was just so frustrating. That is way too long for anyone to have to suffer.

Julie also had to change her diet and cut out all inflammatory foods such as gluten, grains, dairy, sugar, processed foods, and nightshades. That is where a food sensitivity test would also be highly beneficial. I know many people from over the years that have lowered their antibodies just by removing gluten from their diet. Many people do very well on autoimmune paleo diets or as mentioned, an anti-inflammatory diet. According to endocrineweb.com in 2014, 14 million people have a thyroid disorder in the United States. This is why it is so important to look into iodine supplementation for these disorders or to possibly prevent them from happening. Many doctors in my experience know very little about it or what they do know is not accurate. They tend to spread fear about it and definitely have tried to deter Julie from taking it. It is needed for every cell of the body.

According to endocrineweb.com in 2014, 14 million people have a thyroid disorder in the United States.

Women in Japanese cultures do not suffer the same fate that American woman do because Japanese woman usually eat around 13.8 milligrams daily of iodine just in their diet. We also live in Michigan which is part of the "goiter belt" region in the Great Lakes and other areas and I know so many people that have issues like Julie. A friend of ours used to live overseas and she never had any health issues. She then moved to "goiter belt" and now she has Hashimotos. There are so many things that can be said about iodine. This is just an introduction to it. I encourage people to educate themselves on the topic. There are wonderful resources online with Dr. Brownstein, Dr. Flechas, "*Stop the Thyroid Madness,*" and others. There are many books written in great support of it as mentioned above. People healing their auto-immune disorders, their fibrocystic breast disease and the list goes on. It was one of the very best things I ever discovered in helping my wife heal and get her life back in balance.

CELERY JUICE

Social media seems to be exploding with daily posts about celery juice. Maybe you have heard about it, maybe not. But celery juice and its benefits seem to have erupted. It seems to be everywhere! I started researching this and came across a lady who wrote about her own personal benefits in a blog called *Thyroid Yoga*. According to Anthony Williams, the "Medical Medium" who wrote numerous books by the same name and all about this healthy phenomenon that seems to be catching on, like crazy. It seems to be catching on for good reason too!

According to Anthony Williams, celery juice is one of the most powerful super foods you can drink. He recommends just 16 ounces on an empty stomach every morning can transform your health and digestion in as little as one week. Many people with autoimmune diseases almost always suffer with low stomach acid and have difficulty digesting foods. They tend to suffer from leaky gut and other digestive ailments such as bloating and constipation. According to the blog from *Thyroid Yoga (www.thyroid.yoga. com)*, "Celery juice contains compounds called coumarins, that are known to enhance the activities of white blood cells and support the vascular system. It also helps to purify the bloodstream, as mentioned, aids in digestion, reduces blood pressure and clear up skin problems.

Celery is rich in Vitamin A, magnesium, and iron, which all help to nourish the blood. Celery juice is also rich in organic sodium content, meaning it has the ability to dislodge calcium deposits from joints and hold them in solution until they can be eliminated safely from the kidneys. Celery's natural sodium draws out toxic salts from the body from poor quality foods. It replaces them with cluster salts from the celery juice that your body really needs. Cluster salts can systematically flush out toxins, dead pathogens such as viruses and bacteria and pathogenic neurotoxins and debris from every crevice of the body." And this is part of the healing powers of celery juice.

Why juice and not blend? According to *Nutrioned.org/juicing* "The blending process does not extract nutrients from the produce in the same way juicing does. It also gives your body a break when it comes to digestion. By removing the insoluble fiber, it helps the body break down the nutrients faster. Juicing is more favorable for those who have digestive issues." According to http://www.healthline.com, «Juicing contains more concentrated amounts of vitamins and nutrients. Easier absorption of nutrients and easier for digestion and better for the healing process."

I started to do even more research and there are countless stories online and in social media where people have lost weight, they have more energy, better digestion, better sleep, less cravings, and skin issues cleared up. The results appear to be amazing! It is a very inexpensive way to add in something so beneficial for your health. As always, you have to be your own healthcare advocate and see if it resonates with you. Research it and see if it feels right for you, if not, you simply find something else that works for you. I just really like this as it is inexpensive and very easy to incorporate into your life. If you do decide to give it a try, it is recommended that you get a masticating juicer. According to *Healthykitchen101.com* "The masticating juicer has an auger to crush the produce. It separates the pulp and juice by squeezing the produce. The juice runs through the mesh while the pulp will be pushed into a separate container." It sounds to me like more juice is extracted from the produce also. However, if you don't have a juicer, you can use a high-speed blender and then a cheese cloth or nut bag as used for making nut milks like almond butter to strain or some other type of strainer to remove the additional produce.

All you need is one stalk of celery (organic is preferred) as you are trying to get toxins out of the body, not add more in. Just add a bit of filtered water just to help the blades process it, as the stalks are very fibrous. Wash the celery thoroughly, cut into chunks, blend, strain (if using blender), then drink immediately for the most health benefits. It is recommended to do 16 ounces in the morning on an empty stomach. Some individuals will say they had to work their way up to the 16 oz. Even if you can't do it in the morning, you can still do it during the day to get health benefits. It might take some time to get used to as it may be an "acquired taste" for some, while others say it is refreshing. It's just recommended in the morning on an empty stomach for the most health benefits. However, you can still get health benefits at other times too. For more resources, check out the Facebook group: *Celery Juicing Benefits*.

Also check out the Medical Medium's (Anthony Williams) books which include: *Life Changing foods, Thyroid Healing, Liver Rescue* and his original Medical Medium book called *The Secrets Behind Chronic Mystery Illnesses and How to Finally Heal*. I have all of these books and highly recommend them. They are a wealth of knowledge for so many of us trying to heal. So many of these health habits are inexpensive, but also very powerful and work.

THE FEET AND DIET

There are many dietary issues that relate to your foot health. Increased sugar in your diet can lead to diabetes and eventually numbness and burning pain in your feet. Caffeine can also lead to vasoconstriction and decreased blood flow to the feet and toes. A diet that is high in purine can cause an increase in uric acid in the body which will cause gout. Gout is an arthritis usually seen in the big toe joint with symptoms of a red, hot, swollen joint and caused from crystals formed from high uric acid levels. Many foods can trigger an acute gouty attack including ingesting high amounts of red meat, shell fish, cheese, and alcohol. Adding coconut oil to your diet is great for prevention of fungus, yeast and molds to the feet and helping with candida and athlete's feet. Adding 2 tablespoons of Epsom salt and lukewarm water in a bucket and soaking your feet in them for 30 minutes a day will help to rid toxins and bacteria and serves as an excellent detox of the body through your feet. I have a lot of my patients do Epsom salt and water soaks daily and many of them come back when I see them and tell me how much better they feel and how much better their feet look

Caffeine can lead to vasoconstriction and decreased blood flow to the feet and toes.

In addition, I also have a lot of my patients who have swelling in their feet and ankles called edema, to do one simple twenty-minute protocol per day. If you suffer with swelling in your feet, try doing this simple exercise. First, get 2 buckets, trays, or pans that both your feet can fit in and that will also allow enough water to cover your feet. Next, fill one bucket with cold water and the other bucket with warm water. I would then add 2 tablespoons of epsom salt to each bucket. Then stir the salt around to mix with the water and then set your watch timer to 20 minutes. Put your feet in the warm water and soak them for a total of 5 minutes. Then take them out of the warm water and place them in the cold water to soak for a total of 5 minutes. Do the same steps one more time so you have rotated the warm water and the cold water soaks for a total of 20 minutes. Then dry your feet down with a towel. After performing these contrast bath soaks daily for 20 minutes, you will see the amazing results you will see with getting the swelling down from your feet, but also helping you to feel better because of the detox resulting from the epsom salt bath soaks. Your feet will love you for it!

JEFF'S BIG TOE

Jeff came into my office complaining of severe throbbing pain to his left big toe. He said that the pain was like a toothache in his toe and was very hard to walk and sleep because of the pain. He stated that the pain has been present for about 3 days and he was concerned so made an appointment. Upon clinical and radiographic evaluation, the patient was diagnosed with acute gout. He was afraid of needles and didn't want any shots. I educated patient on his condition and also told him about my training in quantum healing and if he was open to trying the quantum healing machine for his painful gout. Since gout is caused from an increase in uric acid and the big toe joint was affected I thought it would make sense to try and neutralize the acid in the joint and decrease the inflammation with the machine. He put his left foot on the gravity wave healing machine for 30 minutes and then I came back into the room.

Upon re-examination I was absolutely floored when I performed range of motion on the big toe joint that there was no pain, compared to the severe pain to big toe upon initial evaluation. In addition, the temperature of the toe joint was cooler and not as hot as it was originally. The patient was absolutely ecstatic and couldn't believe what just happened. I had him stand up and walk and to both of our amazement the toe was pain free. At this point, I was getting excited because the quantum science and machine was actually working and helping people. I am the most skeptical person out there, but at this point I was actually amazed at the results my patients and I were experiencing.

ESSENTIAL OILS

Essential oils are extracts of plants, trees and flowers, condensed into an aromatic oil that is often referred to as aromatherapy. These oils are used for healing in a variety of ways, from diffusers that push the scent into the air, to oils or creams that are used on the body. When massaged into bottom of feet, essential oils absorb into the small blood vessels in the sole within thirty seconds. Within thirty minutes, the oils permeate the cells of the body providing multiple benefits.

For many people, essential oils eliminate the need for some medications which may have unwanted side effects and cause other problems. And best of all, they are not filtered through the liver like oral prescription medications, so if you are immune compromised in any way, essential oils will help you without taxing your body further.

I educate a lot of my patients on the benefits of essential oils for a variety of their health issues. I personally use essential oils on a daily basis. For instance, if I am feeling a little tired with brain fog, I crack out my peppermint essential oil bottle, inhale a little bit of it, and it will immediately make me feel wide awake, alert, energized, allows me to think clearly and become more invigorated. I will also sometimes take my socks and shoes off and rub some of the peppermint essential oil to the soles on the bottom of my feet. Try it out, it does wonders and works a lot better than coffee!

Some common essential oils for feet and their use include:

- **Tea tree oil:** antifungal to relieve athlete's feet, deodorizer, skin softener. Tea tree oil is fairly strong to the touch, you might add a few drops to coconut oil and use as massage oil for the feet. It is ideal for anyone that needs a daily soak or bath.

- **Lavender:** a calming oil that enhances sleep. Rub a few drops to the bottom of your feet before going to sleep. Besides smelling wonderful, lavender is also a great option for wound healing. It can be applied to blisters, sores, and irritated areas of the skin as well as itchy areas on the soles of the feet.

- **Eucalyptus:** anti-bacterial, boosts the immune system. Can be used when feet are tired to help not only relieve aches and pain, but also to address general feelings of exhaustion or fatigue. Best used in a diffuser or steam shower.

- **Peppermint:** natural stimulant, reduces pain or aches in feet. Try a few drops diluted in JoJoba oil for a stimulating foot massage.

- **Frankincense:** very popular in a diffuser for those with infections or cancer. Frankincense has been used for thousands of years to cure disease and sooth the soul.

- **Citrus:** calming, but do not use it on the face as it can cause photo sensitivity.

- **Oregano oil:** highly anti-bacterial. In clinical studies, Oregano oil has killed resistant bacteria such as SARS faster than any other known substance. Dilute in oil and apply to the feet for infections or candida.

- **Thieves blend:** to prevent colds and build immunity.

- **Chamomile:** commonly used in teas to help promote sleep and relaxation. The essential oil can be used to reduce inflammation throughout the body and to also help with reducing any skin damage. Chamomile can be combined with lavender before bedtime to promote both healing as well as natural sleep.

- **Carrier oil:** Such as coconut oil, or almond oil many times should be used with the concentrated essential oils to help dilute them.

KELLY'S NAILS

Kelly came to my office complaining of ugly, thick, and painful fungal nails. She said she was embarrassed wearing open toed shoes because of how ugly and discolored her nails were and also stated that they were painful when she wears shoes because of the pressure. She stated that she didn't want any oral medications as she heard they were bad for the liver and kidney. She also didn't want to go through blood work similar to what her friend had to do to check liver enzymes. I feel that any medication where you have to check liver enzymes before and after use is probably not good for the body. I asked if she was open to holistic natural remedies and she said absolutely.

I then told her to get tea tree oil and coconut oil and mix them together in a 50/50 mixture. I then told her to apply to the top of her affected fungal nails once daily at night using a Q-tip applicator and it will penetrate through the nail plate and go to the nail bed to get rid of fungus, yeast, and mold. A lot of fungal nails can be a combination of any of these and important to address them or the nails will never improve and clear. I then saw the patient one month later, and her fungal nails were almost completely clear. The patient was so happy and excited and amazed on how good the tea tree oil and coconut oil combination worked on her fungal nails and most importantly how much money she saved.

I have seen so many of my patients benefit from use and implementation of essential oils and why I believe they are a great holistic and safe, effective way for people to try. I have found that combination of different essential oils help with different problems and why I carry different essential oil roller balls I mixed with me where ever I go to help prevent me from getting sick, help me if I have any pain and need immediate pain relief, help me to stay alert and oriented, help me to relax and stay grounded and able to sleep.

CBD OILS

CBD is short for cannabinoil derived from the hemp plant. CBD is only one of the 100 known cannabinoils with healing benefits found in the hemp plant. The body contains a natural endocannabinoid system with receptors placed throughout the body–including the brain. Unlike most receptors that can only communicate in one direction, endocannabinoid receptors engage in two-way communications, allowing the cells to talk to each other. This exchange gives information about the body and then directs the CBD to the areas that require calming. Endocannabinoids are especially powerful in reducing inflammation and calming the mind. Research has proven that meditation and calming the mind have anti-inflammatory responses, so CBD is able to reduce inflammation from both the mind and body.

CBD is gaining a lot of visibility and validity in the US with new laws that allow the sale of hemp products. Misconceptions about the plant inspired laws that linked CBD to marijuana, however CBD is the *non-psychotropic* oil from hemp plants, although some dispensaries sell CBD with THC which is the psychotropic component. That being said, the CBD that is most effective for general health to reduce inflammation is over the counter, high quality CBD. In my practice, I dispense CBD oil that has 0% THC which is lab tested and certified. I prefer patients to use CBD without any traces of THC (the psychogenic component) as the THC can be detected in blood tests if CBD oil with THC is being used.

Misconceptions about the plant inspired laws that linked CBD to marijuana, however CBD is the *non-psychotropic* oil from hemp plants.

CBD HELPS DAN

Dan, a sixty-nine year old white male came to my office and was suffering with chronic foot pain, knee pain as well as burning, numbness and pain in both of his feet especially at night time when he went to bed. He seen 7 specialty doctors before coming to my office as a last resort and final opinion. Upon examination and radiographic findings, I discovered he had misalignment in his feet. This misalignment was attributing to his knee and foot pain and was causing compression of the main nerve going into his feet (posterior tibial nerve). After correcting the root cause of his problems, he was starting to get improvement in his painful symptoms. The patient was still having some of his symptoms, so I implemented a regimen of daily sublingual CBD oil drops and application of topical CBD pain cream. The patient noticed an improvement each week and after 4 weeks was completely pain free of both his knee and foot pain and also had no more burning or numbness in his feet. The patient was so appreciative and was very emotional after I helped him get his life back.

CBD HELPS MY DOG BO

CBD oil is also very effective for your furry friends. I had a personal experience recently with the efficacy of CBD oil in helping my ten years old blonde lab dog named Bo. My dog started to limp and I noticed it worsening daily. Then one morning I was getting ready to feed him and noticed he wasn't able to put any weight on his right hind leg. I was so concerned and worried and made an appointment immediately for him to see a veterinarian. I took him to the vet and they said that he had a partial tear to his cruciate ligament to his knee. They wanted to do surgery on him and I didn't feel very comfortable with surgery for him especially since he had to be put totally under for anesthesia and I was concerned about the risks especially since he was so old. I was also afraid of Bo having surgery, since my last dog, Jack, who was also a Lab, had an elective surgery to remove a benign mass and it was the last time I saw him. It brought back flashbacks.

My wife, son, and I went to the movie theater to see a movie while he was having his surgery and while in the theater I received a voicemail from the vet. I assumed it was just that they were giving me a heads up that the surgery went well, and Jack was doing fine. However, the voicemail said that I have to call them immediately about Jack. My stomach felt nauseous and my heart was going a hundred miles an hour as I stepped out in the hallway and called them. I still remember the call to this day and remember falling to my knees and crying in the hallway of the movie theater not believing what I just heard from the vet. They told me that Jack had cancer throughout his entire body and they recommended we euthanize him. I was in shock and didn't know what to say. They told me to come right away and I remember having to get my wife and son out of the movie theater and said we have to go the vet now. They saw the tears on my face and I had to tell them what they said about Jack. It was one of the most traumatizing days I could remember especially losing a member of our family in such an unexpected way.

After leaving the vet with Bo, I wanted to do more research online about his cruciate ligament and see if there were some holistic or alternative treatments we can try to help heal him and get him to walk. I read a lot of testimonials from other pet owners who had dogs with similar issues and how they were able to heal them without surgery. Since I was seeing improvements in my patients with the CBD oil drops and CBD pain cream, I thought I would use on Bo as well. I contacted the CBD company and asked them if it would be ok to use on my dog and they said absolutely. They had a lot of people who had great results using CBD oil for their pets with pain and inflammation and was very safe. I would then add some drops of CBD oil to my dog's food in the morning each day and also rubbed CBD pain cream to his knee each day.

I noticed after a few days he was getting around a lot better and starting to put a little more pressure on his back-hind leg. After 1 week of using the CBD drops and CBD pain cream, Bo was able to actually walk and put full weight and pressure on his back leg with the cruciate ligament injury. I was absolutely amazed and so happy that he was doing a lot better and will not have to go through surgery. I still continue to give him the drops and cream and he is doing great. I am a firm believer in holistic and natural alternative remedies to help with healing. My dog Bo is a prime example on how holistic alternative treatments can help with healing and overall health wellness.

These are very inexpensive and easy habits you can incorporate into your daily life. By following these simple health habits, it can truly make a life changing impact for your health.

My wife and I have been implementing all of these healthy habits into our daily routines and it has made a massive difference in our health. This is precisely why I want to share them, so it can make a huge difference in their lives as well. These are just guidelines to go by in sharing our personal experiences, but it is always important to be your own health advocate.

We are currently living in a society that is very health conscious and more open to alternative and holistic medicine implementation into our lives. *Whole Foot Revolution* is bringing awareness to the most neglected and ignored part of our body, yet the most important with regards to healing of our mind, body, and soul. Our feet are a true mirror to our body and overall health. What's going on with our feet tells us what's going on with the rest of our body. If we are proactive and take care of our foot health, our body health and wellness will be excellent. Most importantly is for us to be healthy and maintain health in order to avoid problems and complications later in life. We as a society, don't even think of our feet and its relation to our health unless you are suffering with foot pain.

We as a society, don't even think of our feet and its relation to our health unless you are suffering with foot pain.

As I stated earlier, our feet are the true foundation to our entire body. They provide information about health and illness throughout our whole body. They are the most neglected and ignored part of our body. When our feet hurt, we hurt all over. Through my training in Western medicine and my in-depth exploration and training in Eastern medicine, I find it imperative in my office practice to incorporate both philosophies and techniques for whole-body health and wellness healing. *Whole Foot Revolution* takes you through the true gift and miracles of our feet, the importance of our feet and foot health to our overall health and well-being, and state-of-the-art treatment approaches using both Western medicine and Eastern medicine principles for reclaiming our mind, body, and sole!

CHAPTER 8

PUTTING SHOES
ON THE WORLD

And forget not that the earth delights
to feel your bare feet and the winds
long to play with your hair.
- Kahlil Gibran

MY SON'S STORY

I still remember to this day one of the stories that I will never forget from when I started helping people with the Shoe Pantry Plus. I remember it because it was so heart breaking yet so heart lifting at the same time. My son Evan who was 12 years old at the time was helping us distribute new boots and socks for the homeless at the Eastern Market in Detroit, Michigan. I remember it was in the heart of the winter and the temperatures were below freezing and there was a ton of snow on the ground. We had approximately 200 pairs of new boots and new socks that we were going to give out to the homeless. We had stations where we would measure their feet with Brannock devices to get the proper size boot and a pair of socks. I noticed my son Evan was sitting in the corner of the room with tears coming down his face and I went up to him and asked him if he was ok. He told me that he just felt sad to see all these people including children that were homeless and he got very emotional.

I then sat next to my son and told him that we need to be grateful and appreciative every day for having a roof over our head and food to eat. I also told him how we as a society need to all help each other out and give back to those in need as we are all one and all brothers and sisters. I gave my son a big hug and told him I love him and am so proud of him and that his sensitivity and emotions really meant a lot to me in that it showed that he cares. I then told my son, "let's go and help put smile, joy, and happiness on the faces of those people that need our help with new properly fitted boots and socks to keep their feet warm and protected." I am so proud of my son Evan and his love and compassion for those people in need. He has volunteered a lot of his time with our events with the Shoe Pantry Plus and hopefully will pass the torch to continue helping people in need through his children and all future generations.

PJ'S STORY

While we were distributing new boots and socks to the homeless of Detroit at Eastern Market during the frigid cold winter, a gentleman named Paul (nicknamed "PJ") came to my station to get sized and fitted for new boots and socks. My son Evan was right next to me when he came to us. He was a very polite and soft-spoken gentleman. We introduced ourselves to him and he told my son that he appreciates his help and started talking about his son whom he truly missed and hadn't seen in 4 years. He started telling us that he wasn't a good father and started to get into drugs and alcohol after he was in a car accident that really messed up his back. He was never around for his son and family and told my son to never drink alcohol or do drugs because it will eventually screw up his entire life. He started talking to my son and in a way felt like he was trying to talk to his son through my son. He was telling him all the wrong things he did and for my son not to do them and told him how he ended up homeless and on the streets.

After we measured his feet and gave him his new boots and pair of socks, he was so happy and excited and so appreciative. He started walking back and forth with his new boots and socks and told my son and I that this was his first new pair of boots that he ever owned. I couldn't believe it, and you can tell that my son Evan was even a little in shock. He gave me a hug and thanked me numerous times and also gave my son Evan a big long hug and as he was hugging my son there were tears coming down from the face of PJ and told my son "I love you" and my son told him "I love you too PJ." I started to choke up and tears came down my face and hugged PJ again and told him that I loved him and to keep the faith as one day he will reunite with his son and family. I still remember PJ to this day and hope he was doing well. When PJ left, my son told me if I noticed that PJ had no socks on and that his boots had holes and open flaps at the toes and would flap up and down when he walked. My son was in absolute shock especially with the brutal cold weather temperatures and snow on the ground here in Detroit. I told him that I noticed it and am so glad that we helped him out and know that now he is able to get around with his feet being warm and protected with his new boots and socks. In other words, we helped PJ get back on his feet and most importantly gave him love and compassion and faith in humanity with him knowing that there are people that truly care for him.

I will always remember PJ's story because it was a bonding I will always remember with my son Evan on how grateful and blessed we should be to have a pair of boots and socks to wear and how important it is to help give back to those that may need our help in times of crisis. Giving is truly the secret to a peaceful soul. This experience I had with my son is beyond words and one that I will cherish forever. I appreciate having the privilege of meeting PJ and allowing my son and I to have this experience. I love my son more than what words can describe.

LAKESHA'S STORY

In the beginning of the school year Shoe Pantry Plus went to a middle school in Detroit to distribute brand new shoes and socks to low income children in need. We were also helped by some former Detroit Lions players to distribute brand new shoes, socks, and backpacks to the children. The kids were so excited and appreciative. While fitting the kids with their new shoes and socks, a young sweet girl with braids came up to me and wanted to know if I had a bigger size shoe as the one she had was too tight on her. I then asked her to show me her shoes and wanted to see how they fit. When she gave them to me, I checked inside the shoes and noticed that there was paper that was stuffed in the toebox. I then took the paper out and she tried them on again and they fit perfectly. She didn't realize there was paper in the shoe when she originally tried them on and she told me that she never owned a new pair of shoes and didn't know there is paper inside the shoes. This was her first new pair of shoes, and she told me that she liked the way they smelled and after I put them on her, she started to run around the room in happiness and joy. This put such a smile on my face and made me feel so good to be able to give someone their first new pair of shoes that they ever owned and most importantly put a smile on their face and make them feel good about themselves.

JIM'S STORY

I remember my Shoe Pantry Plus going to help out the veterans in honor of Veteran's Day at a shelter for homeless in Detroit, Michigan. While out at the shelter there were many veterans that were so appreciative for us to be there and honor them for their service to our country. In speaking with a lot of the veterans, they told me that they don't feel like their appreciated in today's society. Many told me some of their stories while serving in the armed services and how they lost a lot of their friends in battle. A good majority of the homeless veterans I spoke with suffered from post-traumatic stress disorder (PTSD). One gentleman I spoke with named Jim, served in the Vietnam War. He had a baseball cap on that read Vietnam War Veteran. He told me that he was married and just had a newborn baby boy before he was sent out to Vietnam. He said that when he went back to his wife and son after the Vietnam War he was never the same.

He said that he could never recover from all the terrifying things he witnessed while in the Vietnam War. He couldn't sleep at night and would get up in the middle of the night with cold sweats and shaking and have tons of flashbacks of all his traumatic experiences. While fitting him with his shoes and socks he also told me that he had to drink a lot of alcohol to numb up his pain and memories that he suffered when he came back from the war. He said he tried getting professional help, but it didn't work for him and then eventually got so bad that he eventually abandoned his wife and son and went to the streets. He said that he has been on the streets for a while and hasn't spoken to his wife or son in such a long time. I felt so sad for him and his family and just how much suffering our veterans have to go through.

I love our veterans and appreciate all they have done to serve and dedicate their lives for our freedom and country. That is why I enjoy doing a little something for them to show my appreciation for their bravery and true heroism they have done for all of us. They are the true heroes and why I called my event for the veterans "Shoes for Heroes" because they are my true heroes and appreciate each and every one of them. This hits home for me, since my father, Norm, served in the US Army during the Vietnam War. He served as a medical physical administrator in the Armed Forces Examining Entrance Station. I introduced my father to him and both shared stories and experiences with each other.

Jim was so appreciative that we came out to pay tribute to the veterans and fitted each one with brand new shoes and socks. He absolutely loved his new shoes and informed my dad and I that nobody has ever done anything nice like this for him ever. He then gave me and my dad a big hug and thanked us both. We thanked him for all his bravery and service to our country and told him that we love him. He started to cry tears of joy and kept thanking us and showing his deep appreciation for us helping him out. I believe we all as human beings need to show our love and compassion towards one another and to embrace in one another and help each other when were in need. These little things can truly make a difference in this world and really give people hope and a feeling of purpose in this world. That is why I created the Shoe Pantry Plus, because I want to get people literally back on their feet and I believe everyone deserves a new pair of shoes and socks that fits them perfect just like the perfect human being they are. Let's help spread love, compassion, joy and happiness in this world one foot and one step at a time.

The *Whole Foot Revolution* isn't just about healing the mind, body, and soul through our feet, but also helping spread love and compassion throughout this world by putting new shoes and socks on people's feet that are in need and help them to get back on their feet and know there are people that care and that we are all "one" in this world. Let's help to spread positivity and eliminate judgement towards others as you never know what people's real stories are and we all come from all walks of life but are all one.

YOUTH FOOTBALL CAMP

In the summer, the Shoe Pantry Plus helped participate in a summer football camp for youth kids of Detroit headed by NFL All-Pro and Detroit Lions player, Lomas Brown Jr., along with some other NFL Players. While we were there, we measured and sized every kid that participated in the youth football camp utilizing Brannock devices. One thing that I found to be very interesting, is that when I spoke with a lot of the kids, they didn't know their shoe sizes. In addition, when I asked them if they ever had their feet measured and sized for shoes, a great majority of them said that they never had their feet measured. While I was measuring their feet, I noticed something very interesting. A lot of these young kids were wearing cleat shoes that were one and even up to 2 sizes too small or too big for their actual shoe size. When I asked them if they had pain in their feet when they played football, a lot of the kids said yes, but thought it was normal and just played through the pain. A good amount of the kids told me that they were wearing hand me down cleats from their older brother because their parents couldn't afford to buy them new cleats.

This was so heart breaking for me, especially because many of these kids said this was their first new pair of cleats they ever wore. I also wanted to educate the kids and their parents on the importance of proper fitting shoes and importance of having their feet measured. Not only will this prevent foot problems and pain in other parts of the body like the ankles, knees, hips, and back, but it will help with overall performance on the field and minimize sports injuries. The best feeling ever was when these children received their proper sized football cleats and tried them on, they said that their feet did not hurt for the first-time playing football. A lot of them went running down the football field with their new cleats and were so happy and excited and said they were able to run a lot faster and best of all have no pain in their feet.

HOMELESS IN HOLLYWOOD

I flew out to California from Detroit to see my true idol and someone whom I love, admire and respect for all the good works and positivity she spreads throughout this world. That person is Ellen Degeneres and I was so excited at the opportunity to be in her audience and see her live on her *Ellen Degeneres Show*. While I was out in California, I wanted to help give back to the homeless on the streets of LA and Hollywood since I heard from my friend that there was a big homeless problem out in that particular area. He told me there were many people including families that had tents and were lined up along the streets. I shipped some new shoes and socks out to my friend's house in LA/Hollywood area and we were going to help distribute them to those homeless people on the streets. We drove around the area and met so many interesting people on the streets. I told them I was the "Sole Doctor" from Detroit and was visiting from Detroit to help distribute brand new shoes and socks to them. Majority of the people were so thankful and appreciative and even had one gentleman that was so happy and excited, he started singing.

It was such an amazing and heart-warming day to help put a smile and make a small difference in people's lives. I remember one gentleman that was on the street with his dog "baby boy" and said he couldn't go to the shelters because they don't allow dogs into the shelter and he didn't want to leave him. The gentleman was so nice and told me he likes to repair bikes. He was so appreciative and gave me a hug and thanked me for the nice shoes and socks. One other thing I remember him saying was that he loved his shoes and "it felt great to know that somebody cares." This really struck a chord with me and made me feel so good, but most importantly made me understand more about these people on the streets are no different than anyone of us, it is just that they fell on bad times or had some situations that got them where they are now. Most importantly I believe we as human beings are all "one" and we all need to know that we are loved and that somebody cares for us.

Love and compassion for each other is what we need to provide in order to make this world a better place. Even the homeless gentleman told me, "If one person helps out another, we wouldn't have as much heart ache in this world." This is one thing I learned while meeting those people on the streets was that they were so surprised that someone wanted to actually help them. There was a lot of hugs, smiles, and appreciation with everyone we gave new shoes and socks to on the streets of Los Angeles and Hollywood. In fact, there was one gentleman that offered his baseball cap to me to show his appreciation for giving him his new shoes and socks. I was so touched and started to tear up because I felt so bad for a lot of these beautiful angels on the streets that just need some help, love and compassion to get them to where they truly need to be in this world.

By showing care and compassion by doing a little something as simple as giving new shoes and socks, these people were ecstatic and just brightened up like the sun and as one lady said made her "feel like a million bucks!" There is no better feeling in the world than to be able to brighten up someone's day and to make them feel special and appreciated. That is why I founded my Shoe Pantry Plus and with more help from people, corporations, and shoe companies, we can help make my goal and mission a reality by helping at least one million people in need through distribution of new shoes and socks to keep their feet warm and protected. And most importantly to help people get back on their feet!

CHAPTER 9

RESOURCES FOR THE SOLE

When our feet hurt, we hurt all over.
–Socrates

REFLEXOLOGY FOR HEALTH & HAPPINESS
By Laura Norman

WHAT IS REFLEXOLOGY?

Reflexology is an ancient healing art re-discovered in the 20th century because of its enormously effective therapeutic benefits. Reflexology is known to reduce stress, improve circulation and detoxification, and aid many health conditions. Many people also report increased energy, clarity and focus.

Regis Philbin, talk show host and entertainer, tells about how Reflexology helped him painlessly pass kidney stones while he was in the hospital, saving him from having to go "under the knife."

HOW DOES REFLEXOLOGY WORK?

Reflexologists use specially designed thumb, finger and hand techniques to facilitate relaxation and rejuvenate the entire body. Reflexology involves the gentle and skillful stimulation of the nervous, lymphatic, endocrine, digestive, respiratory, cardiovascular and reproductive systems, as well as balancing the subtle energy flow within the body. Results are achieved by applying pressure to specific reflex areas on the feet, hands, ears and face that correspond to all of the organs, glands and other parts of the body. You relax as your body is empowered to cleanse itself of impurities, restore balance, and promote a general sense of well-being.

John, a CPA who works long hours, especially during tax season, came to see me. "I need all the sleep I can get. But I often had a lot of trouble falling asleep and staying asleep. That is, until I found Laura Norman Holistic Reflexology. Now I fall asleep easily and sleep through the night. Thank you, Laura."

WHAT HEALTH PROBLEMS CAN BENEFIT FROM REFLEXOLOGY?

Scientific studies have confirmed what thousands of clients report. With regular sessions Reflexology has been shown to be effective for headaches/migraines, allergies, boosting the immune system, digestive issues, detoxification, women's issues including PMS, infertility, discomforts of pregnancy, birth and menopause, neck, shoulder and back pain, prostate issues, allergies, fatigue and addictive behaviors such as alcoholism, drug abuse, smoking and overeating, Bell's Palsy and other nervous system conditions.

A happy Manhattan client of mine shared, "I suffered with chronic headaches for more than three years. This is the first therapy that has worked for me. I only wish I had heard about it sooner!"

Numerous clients have also had success with releasing excess weight. Many of us overeat due to stress and tension. Reflexology's number one benefit is profound relaxation and is a more positive way to nurture yourself and help make better choices about food. Reflexologists stimulate points on the feet, hands, face and ears corresponding to various glands, organs and systems for weight management. For example:

- Thyroid: Balances metabolism

- Adrenal Glands: Increases energy to burn calories

- Hypothalamus Gland: Controls appetite

- Pituitary Gland: Regulates hormone secretions, including endorphins

- Solar Plexus/Diaphragm: Reduces stress and relaxes breathing

- Digestive/Urinary systems: Stimulates elimination

- Pancreas: Normalizes blood sugar levels

The benefits are extensive and unique for each person. Reflexology is a wonderful way to improve health and well-being and empower you to connect to your greatness.

WHO CAN HAVE A REFLEXOLOGY SESSION?

Reflexology is beneficial to people of all ages, including babies and children, teens and adults, students, seniors, patients in hospice (and their families), artists, professionals, athletes and many more.

Dr Mehmet Oz, well-known cardiologist and a strong proponent of Reflexology, recommends Reflexology for his patients, both pre- and post-surgery.

HOW MANY SESSIONS DOES IT NORMALLY TAKE TO RESOLVE A HEALTH ISSUE?

Clients report they feel better after their first session, and there are more cumulative effects after a series of sessions. Results vary with each individual, and how open and willing they are to let go of their health issue(s) and allow their wellness. Reflexology brings the body into balance/homeostasis, assisting the body/mind to heal itself.

One of my clients and her husband had seen several specialists and experienced several miscarriages over the years in their attempt to have a child. Then, after her seventh reflexology session with me, they found out they were pregnant! She came in for sessions every week throughout her pregnancy and held the vision of having her baby girl in her arms. One day she breathlessly called to tell me "My dream came true. I have my baby girl in my arms right now!"

WHAT DO PEOPLE EXPERIENCE DURING AND AFTER A REFLEXOLOGY SESSION?

Imagine removing just your shoes and socks, lying comfortably on a cushy massage table in a dimly lit room, sounds of music and nature softly playing around you, fragrances of lavender and sandalwood calming your senses. In just these first few moments you start to relax as you begin your profound experience with Reflexology.

As your practitioner gently, but firmly, applies pressure to specific reflex areas that correspond to each part of your body, you drift off into a state of restful awareness or peaceful sleep. At the conclusion of your session you leave feeling relaxed, refreshed and energized yet calm, clear and at peace.

A client I see regularly has arthritis and suffered from achiness and low back pain on and off for many years. Many times it was painful just to lie down. "With my reflexology sessions," she told me, "I can now lie down, and get up, without that stiffness and nagging pain."

Many clients say they feel like they are in a hypnotic trance or dreamlike state, and they frequently do fall asleep. People notice symptoms diminishing and/or disappearing as their health improves. They experience a new inner strength, greater clarity and focus, increased energy, are more effective at work, and their relationships benefit from their increased sense of calm, patience and compassion.

Linda, a mother of two, came to me for sessions because she was looking for a new way to support and nurture her family, especially her son who was asthmatic. After Linda experienced Reflexology with me, read my book and watched my DVD, she began working on her son. Linda is convinced that Reflexology has contributed greatly to alleviating her child's asthma symptoms, as well as her own anxiety.

HOW IS REFLEXOLOGY DIFFERENT FROM MASSAGE?

- Reflexology is non-invasive, i.e., you remain clothed. Only the feet, hands and face are exposed, so you can feel safe and secure throughout the session

- You remain on your back throughout a Reflexology session, maintaining the flow of the session, so you can completely relax (and often fall asleep!)

- Reflexology is time-efficient because there is no undressing/dressing or showering

- Reflexologists can do more sessions in a day and still feel energized when they are done.

- Massage works through the musculature of the entire body, using methods of stroking to restore metabolic balance within the soft tissue. Reflexology employs fine thumb and finger techniques on specific reflex points on the feet, hands, face and ears that can affect all parts of the body, including internal organs and glands.

- Reflexology works predominantly through the nervous system, utilizing subtle energy pathways to optimize how your body functions. Energy pathways are opened up, order and harmony are restored. Your body returns to its natural rhythms as your body, mind and spirit are brought back into balance.

WHY WOULD SOMEONE CHOOSE TO BECOME A REFLEXOLOGIST?

Reflexology is a career choice that promises a sole-to-soul connection between the practitioner and recipient. It's very appealing for anyone choosing to have healing techniques literally at their fingertips. It is a career grounded in the premise that we each have the ability to hear our own inner voice when we allow ourselves to relax and receive. And a career that offers enhanced earning potential and flexible hours, and that opens the door to a life of providing healing and wellness to others.

People from all walks of life who are caring, compassionate and have a desire to help others choose to become Reflexologists. Among the thousands of Reflexologists we have trained are dancers, massage therapists, corporate executives, pilots, chiropractors, carpenters, teachers, acupuncturists, accountants, physical therapists, nurses, estheticians, nail techs, empty nesters and many more choosing to follow a new path or expand their services.

Being a Reflexologist is rewarding in so many different ways. I am thrilled and feel fulfilled each time someone who comes in stressed, anxious, exhausted or in pain leaves feeling calm, relaxed, energized, free of pain.

My Method of Holistic Reflexology empowers the practitioner and their client by addressing the whole person – physically, mentally, emotionally and spiritually. My training program's attention to the spiritual aspects of healing is what drew Debbie Shields and others like her to enroll in our program. Debbie described her training as "absolutely life-transforming!" The hands-on training and the supportive, nurturing class environment she experienced helped Debbie perfect her art. The results she witnesses in her clients "are absolutely amazing!"

Anyone can start right now to "touch somebody's life." Make the choice to live a life both personally and professionally that speaks to your higher self and your loving, caring desire to make a profound contribution to others.

CAN REFLEXOLOGISTS DIAGNOSE HEALTH ISSUES IN MY BODY WHEN WORKING ON MY FEET?

Only physicians, podiatrists and other medical professionals are legally allowed to diagnose health issues. Reflexologists facilitate healing and wellness once the client tells them where they are feeling discomfort, pain, or an imbalance or after they have been diagnosed by a medical professional.

DOES TENDERNESS IN MY FEET CORRESPOND TO A HEALTH ISSUE IN MY BODY?

In many cases tenderness is due to tension or tightness locally on the foot. Tenderness can be caused by a structural issue like bunions or hammertoes. Poor-fitting shoes may irritate the feet. A person's gait may be putting stress on a section of the foot. And, it may be a health issue or stress and tension in the corresponding part of the body, as confirmed by the client or diagnosed by a medical professional.

Author's Note: Laura Norman, author of the best-selling book *Feet First: A Guide to Foot Reflexology*, is a world-renowned authority and educator in Reflexology. She offers comprehensive training programs in New York City, South Florida and The Berkshires in the Laura Norman Method of Holistic Reflexology, which supports clients physically, mentally, emotionally and spiritually. Her holistic method combines Foot, Hand, Ear and Face Reflexology with Inspired Life Coaching to empower clients to improve their health, trust their inspirations and realize their dreams. I attended one of her classes and Laura was kind enough to talk with me personally about the power of Reflexology.

REFLEXOLOGY TRAINING PROGRAMS/ LAURA NORMAN
www.lauranorman.com
classes@lauranorman.com
212-532-4404/561-272-1220

WHAT IS TCM?

Grandmaster Nan Lu—Traditional Chinese Medicine World Foundation

A PATHWAY TO THE LIFE YOU WANT

TCM, or Traditional Chinese Medicine, is a profound pathway to create the life you truly want to live, the life you were born to live. It's a timeless bridge that can initiate and support change and growth in any and every life dimension: physical, mental, emotional, and spiritual.

An Ancient yet Completely Modern Healing System

TCM has the power to unlock your true potential and help you develop and use your own unique gifts and talents. Its insightful wisdom and ability to understand and address individual health needs empowers each person with a way to unite body, mind, and spirit—the foundation for lasting, authentic health. TCM teaches you how to live a life of balance, wellness, and harmony.

It's true that TCM is one of the oldest healing systems on the planet. It has actually been in continuous practice for thousands of years. How can something so old still work for people living today—in your life?

TCM can be effectively applied to help heal anyone and any health issue no matter what year it is because it's rooted in unchanging natural law, which has its source beyond time. This unique paradigm of medicine grew out of penetrating observation of how everything in our reality functions at the deepest, invisible levels and interacts with the surface or visible physical levels. It's a medicine of extraordinary relationships. Every TCM principle, theory, and healing practice reflects and harmonizes with the relationships that exist within natural law

FOUR KEY TCM PRINCIPLES

1. Your body is an integrated whole. Each and every structure in your body is an integral and necessary part of the whole. Along with your mind, emotions, and spirit, your physical body structures form a miraculously complex, interrelated system that is powered by life force, or energy.

2. You are completely connected to nature. Changes in nature are always reflected in your body. TCM factors in the particular season, geographical location, time of day, as well as your age, genetics, and the condition of your body when looking at your health issues.

3. You were born with a natural self-healing ability. Your body is a microcosm that reflects the macrocosm. Think about it: nature has a regenerative capacity, and so do you. Sometimes, this ability may appear to be lost or difficult to access. In most cases, it is never completely gone.

4. Prevention is the best cure. Do you know your body is continually revealing signs about the state of your health? Let's face it, it's common to ignore these signs or symptoms until something more complicated arises. TCM teaches you how to interpret what your body is telling you.

KIDNEY/BLADDER HEALTH

According to Traditional Chinese Medicine, the Kidney is the powerhouse of the body, supplying reserve energy to any organ running low on Qi. Its partner organ is the Bladder.

The season associated with the Kidney is the Winter so it's especially important to slow down and conserve energy by getting more rest!

The Kidney stores reserve energy called "pre-natal Qi" inherited from your parents. When another organ is low on energy, the Kidney sends it an extra Qi boost from this inheritance.

The ears are the sensory organs related to the Kidney. Any ear problems, such as deafness, tinnitus, or ear infections are a signal from your body that the Kidney's energy needs extra support.

The bone is the tissue associated with the Kidney. If the Kidney's energy is low, you may have symptoms such as osteoporosis, dental issues, or developmental issues.

The taste that corresponds to and supports the Kidney is salt, according to the Five Element theory. Craving salt? Listen to your Kidney and have a salty snack!

Fear is the emotion associated with the Kidney. If you often have severe panic attacks, anxiety, and fear, your body may be trying to tell you that Kidney energy is running low or is imbalanced.

FOODS TO SUPPORT KIDNEY HEALTH

Many foods have an essence that resonates with the Kidney. You may crave seafood, beans or bone soup. These are all foods that build strong Kidney function. Listen to the body, and eat what you are in the "mood" for.

SIMPLE TIPS FOR EVERYDAY KIDNEY HEALTH

Some ways to support your Kidney's energy:

Stomp your feet, slowly and with flat feet, for about 5 minutes a day. This stimulates your Kidney's energy as the feet are associated with the Kidney and Bladder meridians, which run through the heel and to the sole of the foot.

Rub your ears for several minutes a day. This simple massage strengthens Kidney function, as the ears are connected energetically to the Kidney organ and meridian.

Stop energy drains! Conserve your energy by sleeping before midnight, resting when you're tired, and giving yourself permission to take a break and de-stress.

ACUPRESSURE FOR KIDNEY HEALTH

Rub the acupressure point called "Yongquan" or "Gushing Spring" (Kidney 1) which stimulates a key point on the Kidney channel. It may be sore, but this means you're hitting the right spot to stimulate your body's energy foundation and relieve symptoms such as night sweats, hot flashes, tinnitus, hypertension, insomnia, anxiety, and headaches.

The yongquan is located at the exact center of the bottom of each foot. Starting with your left foot, massage this point as deeply as comfortable using your thumb or even a tennis ball—anything you have on hand.

A SIMPLE FOOTBATH TO BUILD KIDNEY ENERGY

Pào jiāo is a footbath. In Chinese, pào means "to soak" and jiāo means "to pour water on." You can also get the same effect of this traditional Chinese healing technique by taking a full bath and keeping your feet immersed in the water. In the past, full hot baths were considered a rare luxury in China. So a simple foot-bath served the purpose.

Over the millennia, TCM practitioners have created numerous self-healing techniques like pào jiāo, as well as energy practices like Qigong. These techniques are based on their deep under-standing of Qi and how it flows through the body's invisible en-ergy network, called meridians. These practitioners realized that good health depends on three factors. An person must have a good amount of Qi, his or her Qi must flow freely through the meridians, and the five major organ pairs must work in harmony.

Several key Kidney acupoints are located on the bottom of the feet and on the inside of the ankles. Pào jiāo warms these acu-points and stimulates the Kidney organ system. This helps build the Kidney's energetic function, or tasks it performs at the in-visible level of energy. The Kidney organ system is responsible for storing and providing Qi over your entire lifetime! It helps maintain your bones, teeth and ears. It also nourishes the hair on your head.

Acupoints of the Bladder, the Kidney's organ partner, also run through the feet. They are located along the outside of each foot, in line with the little toe. The Bladder's energetic function is to remove water by transforming Qi in the body.

Both the Kidney and Bladder need enough Qi to carry out their physical and energetic responsibilities. A lack of Qi can affect their function and the health of the body as a whole. When practiced on a regular basis, techniques like pào jiāo and Qigong help to build the Qi of the related organs.

Practice pào jiāo at home.

Immerse your feet in warm water, making sure your ankles are covered. Soak for at least fifteen minutes a day. Relax and enjoy yourself—you're enhancing your health!

TCM HEALTH TIP: FOOT MASSAGE

Massage is a great remedy for sore, tired feet. It also helps calm the mind and release feelings of anger and nervous tension due to stress.

Energy pathways called meridians run through your feet. One point on the Liver meridian, called Taichong, is beneficial for releasing Liver Qi stagnation. It is located on top of your foot where the big toe bone meets the second toe bone (about an inch back from the skin between these toes). Using your thumb, press and massage this spot on both feet (the meridians are on both sides of your body). You can also rub with your thumb moving forward along the inside of the big toe. If it's sore, you're hitting all the right spots! You are unblocking your Liver Qi. Rub this area every day.

Traditional Chinese Medicine World Foundation

Grandmaster Nan Lu

www.tcmworld.org 212-274-1079

TONG REN TECHNIQUE – TOM TAM

Tong Ren is an energy healing therapy developed by Tom Tam as an integral part of the Tom Tam Healing System.

It is based on the premise that illness is related to interruptions, or blockages, in the body's natural flow of: blood, neural bioelectricity, blood, hormones and chi (life force energy). Most blockages can be manually identified along the spine where they inhibit the activity of the central nervous system.

Tong Ren utilizes a universal energy source—the "collective unconscious," in Jungian terms—to remove a patient's blockages and restore the body's natural ability to heal, even when illnesses are chronic, debilitating, or otherwise untreatable.

Because no physical contact is involved or necessary, Tong Ren is often practiced as distance healing. In a typical session, the Tong Ren practitioner uses a lightweight, magnetic hammer to tap specific points on a small anatomical model of the human body, which serves as an energetic representation of the patient.

The practitioner directs chi to blockage points corresponding to the patient's condition, which breaks down resistance in those areas. As blood flow, neural transmission, and hormone reception are restored, the body is then able to heal.

Tong Ren integrates elements of Medical Science and Traditional Chinese Medicine (TCM) to create a powerful new healing modality.

HISTORY OF TONG REN

Tong in Chinese means bronze; Ren means man or human. Tong Ren can be translated as 'bronze man'. In the Sung Dynasty (1023 AD), Emperor Ren Zhong Sung summoned the highest medical faculty of the Empire to write up the "New Bronze Man's Points of Acupuncture Diagram and Note". Dr. Wang Wei-yi was responsible for designing the acupuncture bronze man (human figure made by bronze). In 1027 AD, two identical bronze men were made, which were named Tong Ren (meaning "bronze man" in Chinese). Tong Ren Healing is an important component of the Tom Tam healing system. To commemorate the Traditional Chinese Medicine (TCM) pioneers for their invaluable contribution to the world on the medical front, "Tong Ren Healing", an energy healing system developed by Tam was named after the acupuncture figure created by the TCM forerunners.

Tong Ren healing is becoming increasingly popular and widespread. Worldwide, and on a daily basis, people with serious illnesses are treated by Tong Ren therapists. Countless patients benefit from and are healed by Tong Ren Therapy. Each Tong Ren therapist has his/her own way of healing people. The effectiveness of the healing is high, and the cost is low. Tong Ren Therapy is extremely easy to learn. Basically, there are a few major techniques

1. Magnetic Hammer

2. Laser Beam

MAGNETIC HAMMER

The magnetic hammer technique is the primary method used in Tong Ren Guinea Pig Classes for group healing. We use the hammer to tap points on the doll for about 10- 15 minutes. Patients typically describe feeling inner warmth, tingling, movement, or sensation; this tends to be the case regardless of which technique is used. Patients can tap the doll for self-healing, but they will gain more benefit if someone else taps for them; this allows the patient to relax more fully in order to receive the healing energy.

With the hammer technique, the first step is to locate the points on the doll. The beginner can follow the healing chart in our text book "A Lazy Bum's Healing", then write down the main points and support points on paper or mark the points on the doll. On the healing chart, the main points indicate where the energy is blocked and where the root of the problem is. The support points enhance the effectiveness of the healing and are not mandatory, whereas the main points are.

When we press on a patient's body following the main points from the chart, the patient will usually experience an uncomfortable or painful feeling at these points. In TCM theory these are called the Ouch Points. We need to pay attention to any Ouch Point, or any area where pain is felt. Pain is a signal from the body, which indicates that there is an imbalance or where the Chi is static. For example, when one has liver cancer, we shall find an Ouch Point at T9 on the right-hand side. When a patient has breast cancer, we can easily find an Ouch Point at T4, on the same side as the tumor. Based on many years of practice and experience, I have observed that when a person is diagnosed with a specific condition or disease, they will have an Ouch Point, which corresponds to a certain designated root problem. However, please be careful not to mislead a patient by making a diagnosis according to an Ouch Point. A blockage can sometimes mean just a tight muscle – nothing more, nothing less. Making a diagnosis is the job of medical doctors using specific medical equipment and/or tests. In our healing, we only follow the doctor's diagnosis to find the blockage or reflex points. We never make any diagnosis of a patient's condition.

When we use the hammer technique on the doll for healing, the general order of stimulation is from the top to the bottom, like the natural flow of water. However, when we stimulate the Sky Window area where both the common carotid and vertebral arteries are found, the order of hitting should be from the bottom to the top. This is different from when we are working on the nervous system, because the arteries carry blood upward from the heart to the brain. When we are done with all the points with the hammer technique, we should hit the doll from the top of the head to the bottom of the feet. This allows for the clearing of the Chi in the whole body before we finish the healing session.

While treating cancer, we should begin by using the hammer on the head of the doll at GV22 and BL6 on both sides. After a couple of minutes, proceed to CR8's which are not on the doll. The two CR8 points are where the ears are. Do this for another couple of minutes, then move on to the points related to the specific cancer(s). When treating multiple cancers, we always start with the primary cancer, even though there may not be any symptoms.

Tong Ren Therapy is based on the power of our mind creating energy for healing. The source of this energy is from the collective unconscious, which is connected to the super conscious. When we practice Tong Ren, the focusing of our mind comes from our subconscious and unconscious – which means, "Just do it". If we make a conscious effort to focus, the focusing comes from our conscious mind, not from the unconscious mind. No one can consciously access one's unconscious mind. The unconscious mind is instinctive and cannot be controlled. Functions of the unconscious mind are automatic reactions. This use of the mind with the hammer technique facilitates the breaking down of blockages, which can then let energy pass within the body freely. With Tong Ren healing, we do not need to think or focus on the breaking down of the blockages, because the thought has already been stored as memory in our subconscious mind.

Using the hammer technique, we hit points on the doll for about 10 to 15 minutes. As a rule this is enough. Patients can hit the doll for self-healing, but the best way is to ask someone else to do it because in this way the patient can be totally relaxed in order to receive the healing energy. A child's mind is purer than an adult's and without resistance. That is why children are more effective when using the hammer technique than most adults. With late stage cancer, daily use of Tong Ren healing is required. With cancer at an early stage, we can use Tong Ren two or three times a week. If the patient wants to do it or have it done on him/her more often, it is all right to do so because there are no side effects with Tong Ren healing. The more you do it, the more you benefit from it.

When we see points on the spine from the Lazy Bum book, e.g. C1, T1, L1, S1, we hit the doll on both side of the points. If C1 Right is specified, for example, then we hit only the right side of C1.

LASER BEAM

Another technique for Tong Ren healing is the use of laser beam on the doll. The laser beam technique represents heat, the building up of Chi to apply radiation onto a tumor, similar to the use of radiation in the hospital. Our concept is that of making the tumor shrink or disappear with heat. When using the laser beam, we point the light to where the tumor is on the doll. The laser beam technique is also helpful for charging one's energy for treating the side effects from radiation and chemotherapy. The method is simple – just put the laser beam onto CV4 or CV6, or in between, where the lower Dantian is located. Basically, the laser beam is used on one spot at a time. However, if the patient or the therapist prefers, more than one laser beam can be pointed at the doll at the same time.

The healing session with the laser beam can be 10 to 20 minutes. Some patients like to have the light on longer. This does not have any side effects. Some cancer patients put the laser on the whole night long, which is fine as long as one does not mind wasting batteries. The use of the laser beam for healing cancer is simple and easy. Just turn the light on and point it onto the tumor area. One can do self-healing and a Tong Ren therapist does not need to be involved. When the light is on, it is best for the patient to be fully relaxed, making the healing more effective. During a healing session, we suggest that the patient does not read anything or watch TV. When using the laser beam on the doll, a patient may feel heat on the face. At the same time, the heat may go towards the area where the tumor is located. This is called Chi running in the body, which is important for healing. Someone may feel an expanding sensation in the chest and feel deeper and or easier breathing. For patients with multiple cancer or with advanced cancer, directing the laser onto the lower dantien of the doll for 10 – 15 minutes will charge the patient with Chi.

In Tong Ren healing, we can use the hammer and laser beam simultaneously. We can use one doll with a laser beam on the tumor area, and another doll with the hammer technique to break down the blockages and to stimulate the support points. In this way, the healing could be more effective in a shorter period of time. We can also use the hammer stimulation first, and then use the laser beam afterward. Each session is about 20 minutes with the combination of the two healing techniques.

ENDORSEMENT FROM TOM TAM

"The human body is a complicated system, yet it is perfect in all its infinite number of calculations and movements. In our body, all the Qi and energy comes from the earth and through our feet. The feet are what grounds us, as it is the root of the body. With such an importance on this root, we have researched and developed new technology to recharge and heal. Dr. Anthony Weinert is very knowledgeable in his field yet is open minded and seeks to combine our theories with his own. In the future of healthcare, both modern and alternative medicines should be combined as one. When reading this book, you will discover many new ideas and new concepts for healing, with a renewed understanding and appreciation of our feet, the very thing that keeps us grounded, rooted, and moving forward into the future medicine."

-TOM TAM

Tong Ren Healing & Quantum Healing
Tom Tam Healing System/ Oriental Culture Institute
www.tomtam.com/ www.tongrenstation.com 617-770-4048

ENDORSEMENT FROM LOMAS BROWN, JR

"Dr Weinert has been a godsend to me, my family and the Lomas Brown Jr Foundation. I was having really bad foot pain from years and years of professional football as an offensive lineman, thru treatment from doc I am living pain free. He is a trusted friend now who I didn't hesitate to start treating my wife and kids with great results, also as a trusted physician he works with my foundation to help promote and service underprivileged kids foot health. I thank Dr Weinert for a pain free way to live...

-Lomas Brown Jr"

OTHER RESOURCES

Stop Feet Pain Fast Institute-
Dr Anthony Weinert www.stopfeetpainfast.com
docfoot@sbcglobal.net
586-751-3338

Dr Weinert's Shoe Pantry Plus 501c3 Non-Profit Organization
www.shoepantryplus.org
248-362-3338

Dr. Anthony Weinert Author Site www.anthonyweinert.com

Happy Feet Radio Podcast- Dr. Anthony Weinert
www.docweinert.com

Chuck Christian-Artwork

Chuckchristian-Designs.com

Quantum physics-Energy Healing on Youtube.com "Dr. Quantum"

CBD (Cannabidiol) Information www.Projectcbd.org

WHOLE FOOT REVOLUTION-DR. WEINERT'S HOLISTIC HEALTH WELLNESS STORE

www.wholefootrevolution.com

Follow Dr Weinert

Facebook: Facebook.com/stopfeetpainfast

Twitter: @stopfeetpain

LinkedIn: Dr. Anthony Weinert

Follow Shoe Pantry Plus

Facebook: Facebook.com/Shoepantryplus/

Twitter: @shoepantryplus

Instagram: @shoepantryplus

DR. ANTHONY WEINERT

Dr. Weinert is a recognized authority and leading foot health expert. Dr. Weinert is the creator and founder of the Stop Feet Pain Fast Institute, a #1 source for fast foot pain relief in Michigan. As one of Michigan's premier podiatric surgeons and philanthropist, Dr. Weinert is known for his caring, educating, and his overall concern for patient care and safety. Dr. Weinert prides himself on his holistic integrative approach to foot care and to life. Where many doctors only treat feet locally, he has the unique gift of being able to link foot problems to other, more comprehensive, underlying conditions in the body. He believes in the philosophy that the foot is the foundation to the entire musculoskeletal system.

Dr. Weinert also served for 8 years as the Chief of Podiatric Medicine & Surgery at Henry Ford Bi-County Hospital located in Michigan. He has published the foot health wellness book, "Stop Feet Pain Fast- A Users Guide to Foot & Ankle Health" and "The Sole Doctor's Guide to Happy and Healthy Feet". Dr. Weinert is also the host of "Happy Feet Radio" which is the first show on iTunes dedicated to foot health and wellness. Dr. Weinert believes in the motto "Happy Feet, Happy Life!"

Dr. Weinert's life mission is to give back by serving and educating others on how to live a healthy and quality filled life. Dr. Weinert is a representative of the Detroit City Council Task Force on Homelessness and a major community advocate. Dr. Weinert established a 501c3 non-profit organization, Shoe Pantry Plus, to provide new shoes, boots, and socks to the homeless, veterans, disabled, and low-income adults and children in the community. The Shoe Pantry Plus organization helps to keep the feet warm and protected to those that are less fortunate. Dr. Weinert and his family enjoy giving back and volunteering for charities around the community.

These qualities make Dr. Weinert the go-to expert and recognized authority for many premier national media outlets, including radio, TV, internet and magazines, when it comes to articles and information on foot health and wellness.

His passion, personality, sensitivity, and bedside manner with his patients is absolutely amazing and relatable to people. His positive energy and love for life is infectious. Dr. Weinert believes in "Changing the world one step at a time".